You Can ...
EXPECT A MIRACLE
Yes YOU Can

Dr John Hinwood
AND FRIENDS

EAM Publishing

You Can Expect A Miracle

Yes YOU Can

Dr John Hinwood
Website: www.expectamiracle.com

Published by
EAM Publishing
PO Box 4125
Forest Lake, Queensland, 4078
Australia
Phone: +61 7 3879 0069
Email: admin@expectamiracle.com

Copyright © 2013 by Dr John Hinwood

All rights reserved. This book may be reproduced and transmitted in this form by any means, electronic or mechanical, including photocopying, recording, or by any information storage and retrieval system.
This book is given to you 're-print rights free'.

Please email this book as a gift to family, friends, colleagues, clients, customers and anybody else who can use a good dose of miracle stories.

ISBN: 978-0-9872805-1-0

Cover design by: idrewdesign

Why not use Drs John & Judy Hinwood as guest speakers for your next conference or seminar?
EXPECT A MIRACLE SCHOOL Pty Ltd

PO Box 4125, Forest Lake 4078, Queensland, AUSTRALIA
Tel: +61 7 3879 0069
Fax: +61 7 3714 9700
Email: info@expectamiracle.com
Website: www.expectamiracle.com

Drs John & Judy Hinwood have an unusual way of changing people's lives. In a journey over the past 26 years they have been handing out a small white card to people they have met. The card has just three words written on it ... **"Expect A Miracle"**. They have handed out over 95,000 cards to people all over the world in the last 26 years. Through this small act of giving the Hinwood's prompt people to think about their own miracles; the small, seemingly insignificant events and moments in people's lives that open the doors to a sense of wonderment and opportunity.

John & Judy Hinwood are sought-after international conference speakers and they run public events all over the world.

As international speakers they inspire their audiences into taking practical action steps to move their lives to new levels. Their perspectives, humour, observations, insights into life and entertaining stories are from the heart and they inspire and motivate people into taking positive action steps.

The inspirational You Can EXPECT A MIRACLE book series are giving many people around the world hope and a good dose of positivity.

Also by Drs John & Judy Hinwood

Expect A Miracle Cards
Expect A Miracle card packs

Live Events
Creating Miracles In Your Life (1 hour)
The Miracle Mindset (2 hours)
Expect A Miracle School (Half Day)
Stop Stress Now (2 hours)
Stress to Strength – The Workshop (2 Days)

Webinars ... Streamed
Creating Miracles in Your Life
The Miracle Mindset
Expect A Miracle School

Books
You Can EXPECT A MIRACLE ... The Book To Change Your Life
You Can EXPECT A MIRACLE ... Yes YOU Can
You Can EXPECT A MIRACLE ... Unexpected Miracles
You Can EXPECT A MIRACLE ... With Chiropractic
You Can EXPECT A MIRACLE ... Insights Into Life
You Can EXPECT A MIRACLE ... 201 Miracle Messages from A to Z
You Can EXPECT AMIRACLE ... 13 Keys to Becoming A Miracle Magnet

Audio Programs ... CD & Streamed
Creating Miracles in Your Life
The Miracle Mindset
Expect A Miracle School

Dr John Hinwood

Online Programs

Stress to Strength Alliance ... Via email and webinar

Stress to Strength ... Powerful Steps – 23 days

Stress to Strength ... Final Keys – 49 days

Stress to Strength Coaching Program

Practitioner Training

Stress to Strength Practitioner ... Certificate IV Training

www.expectamiracle.com

Table Of Contents

Acknowledgements 7
Dedication..9
Foreword 11
Introduction...13

1. MIRACLES OF ATTITUDE

   Expect A Miracle …
   (it is more than a simple card trick).........18

   The Card That Can Put a Twinkle
   in Anyone's Eye 22

   A State Of Expectancy 27

   It's The Miracle Put Inside The Card 29

   Is There A Miracle Waiting For You
   Around The Corner? 31

   Expecting Good and Good is
   Happening 34

2. MIRACLES OF COURAGE

   Expect A Miracle Lou.................................38

   Jumping Off the Story Bridge 41

   I 'Hit the Wall' Six Times In My Life 43

3. MIRACLES OF FAMILY

   Expecting My Miracle Baby......................52

The Power of Family 55
Expect A Miracle is a Great Message .. 57
My Expect A Miracle Card Brings Good Luck.. 58
My Miracle Daughter............................... 60

4. MIRACLES OF FREEDOM

It Was an Unexpected Miracle 64
That Card Made Her Day 66
All The Little Miracles That Surround Me 67

5. MIRACLES OF HEALTH & HEALING

How to Make Lemonade... First You Need Some Lemons............................. 70
Postponing Babe's Suicide: The Mind, Body Connection 84
What You Think About … Comes About 86
The Clenched Fist 89
We Raced Through the Streets Of Lima 91
The Miracle Provider 96

6. MIRACLES OF HOPE

My Miracle Dream................................ 102
A Powerful Tool in Essence 105
New Hope in His Life.............................. 107

Free Hugs 109
Every Day Is A Miracle 111

7. MIRACLES OF LESSONS IN LIFE

I Was At Rock Bottom 114
The Speeding Ticket Miracle 116
Every Day Something Lucky, Fortunate, Miraculous Happens 118
Who Was That Guy? 120
He Assumed a State Of Being 124

8. MIRACLES OF SPORT

My First Rugby International 130
I Didn't Have Any Direction in My Life . 135

9. MIRACLES OF WORK

How Did You Find Me? 138
Put Out the Energy 140
Hit By a Bull 142
Path to Life 147
Sixty Five Million Wheelchairs Needed Globally 149
They Were All Wearing Them 155

Share Your Miracle Stories 160
Visit our Website 162
Looking for a Speaker for Your Next

Conference, Seminar or Workshop? 164
About the Author.. 166
Print Your Own Expect a Miracle Cards . 169
Create Miracles For Others… 172
Share the Gift of a Book 173

Acknowledgements

Thank you to all those friends and colleagues who have continually encouraged me to write more books in this *You Can Expect A Miracle* series.

Thank you to my beautiful wife and best mate of 45 years Judy, who has continually encouraged me to write about my experiences from handing out thousands of Expect A Miracle cards all over the world.

Thank you to all the contributors of such wonderful miracle stories: Peter Amlinger, Joseph Ireano, Tracy Kennedy-Shanks , Paul Marshall, Sally Reidman, Eric Pearl, Eloise Anderson, Louise Monaghan, Heather Fulwider, Simon Austin, Susan Howarth, Rob Gregory, Matteo Capellino, Renee Coltson, Paula Byrnes, Mason Garten, Brett Ireland, Brandon Clift, Berni Ireland, Erika, Cathy Duncan, Maria Carlton, Eric Plaster, Larry Markson, Ann Napper, Adrian Wenban, Tomas Bouda, Duane Alley, Michael Massey, Jenni Gorman, Liam Schubel, Ross McDonald, Shawn Bean, Derek Gallant and Keith Livingstone. They come from many and varied backgrounds, and their stories represent events that have occurred over many years.

The contributors come from Australia, Canada, Czechoslovakia, England, Guam, Israel, Spain, New Zealand, Scotland, Peru, Thailand and the

USA.

Thank you to my Personal Assistant Di Girot, who has typed, edited, retyped and made suggestions during the preparation of the manuscript. Also to my friend John Milne who commented on the content and provided editing support.

Thank you to my editor Geoff Whyte for his creative inspirations, understanding and input in the creation of this book.

Special thanks to Drew of idrewdesign for his creative skill in producing a cover design that reflects the essence of the stories in this book.

I also thank Nyrie Roos, Sean Roach and their team at Publishing Catapult have been invaluable in all facets of creative design with the back cover, layout and production and getting the book published. There have been many versions of numerous areas of the book that have had to be redone several times to get the best possible result. Their perseverance and patience has been greatly appreciated.

This book is dedicated to my amazing parents

Ivy and Jack Hinwood

who believed in miracles, and most of all,

believed in me.

Foreword

Miracles take place every single day, but they may slip right past our awareness if we have not tuned in to their frequency. When we are scouting them out, our awareness is heightened and they appear right before us almost on command because we have correlated our desire with an intended outcome.

When you have your eyeglass prescription updated, as I do yearly, the doctor asks, "Is it better now or was it better before?" as you peer into the machine. The forward and backward clicking of the lenses causes one to think about how we are forever changing in this sense of sight, as well as in all other ways. As we change our lenses, so too does our vision change.

Life can be seen through rose-coloured glasses or through a glass darkly, as the poet states, but we determine the lens we use. For many people, 20/20 vision is only achieved by wearing prescription lenses. The doctor helps us achieve this goal through his or her training and capacity to correct or improve our eyesight. Likewise, our vision involving hindsight, foresight, and insight are visionary mechanisms that occur mentally and spiritually inside of us, and can also be aided by another's prescription. The books we read and the people we meet, to quote Charlie T. Jones, are the significant ingredients to an improved life. If we truly want to move forward and advance toward our destiny, we must work hard to reach that goal. As Jeffrey Gitomer, a student of Charlie T. Jones reminds us, we must work hard at our goal and not just expect the universe to deliver it gift wrapped on our doorstep. We must want it to happen, and then consistently work to make it so.

Miracles are hard work, but they do happen. They take more than wishing. They take physical effort, dedication, persistence, personal initiative, and preparedness before a like-minded universe graces us with the opportunity to see our open niche and to align with a miracle in the making. Our true best self, or what Napoleon Hill calls our higher self, is the key to recognizing this opportunity. Remember to set a goal, reach higher and higher, and then catch that miracle as it travels toward your best self. Much like a salmon swimming upstream, you can achieve your goal, but it does not come without effort.

Be Your Very Best Always,

Judy Williamson

Director of the Napoleon Hill World Learning Centre

Purdue University, Calumet, Indiana, USA

Introduction

In 2008, when Executive Books Inc. in the US published You Can EXPECT A MIRACLE ... The Book To Change Your Life, I was excited that this simple, yet very powerful message would be available in bookstores and online to support the lives of people in many countries. Four months later, the Australian edition was published, and last year the e-book edition became available online with Kindle and Smashwords and from our online store.

At the time of the release of the book, I had personally handed out over 50,000 Expect A Miracle cards to clients and people I'd met all over the world. Four years on, that number of Expect A Miracle cards I have handed out has moved to over 95,000. Who knows how many hundreds of thousands or maybe even millions of cards have been printed by people from around the world who visit the website daily.

In Australia over the past year, on a number of occasions, I have had people give me an Expect A Miracle card. When I have shared with them that I'm 'The Miracle Man' and the cards started with me 26 years ago, they are amazed, and on each occasion the person involved has displayed a wonderful attitude of gratitude.

In the four years since the book has been published in the US and Australia, it has gone to two printings and been available in bookstores across the country. I enjoyed doing many book signings at Angus & Robertson in Australia, and at Borders and Barnes and Noble in the US.

Probably the best thing for me personally is that so many people I give a card to, no matter what their station in life is, turn the card over to find it blank on the back. After a pause, I say, "Would you like a miracle?" They almost always say, "Oh yes!"

The change in state of most individuals on receiving the card, reading the words *Expect A Miracle*, turning the card over to find no name, no advertising, no gimmick, purely a message of hope, is heart-rending to witness. Most people move to an enlivened state of wellbeing after reading these three powerful words. For some, who only show a glimmer of hope that it's possible for their life to be even a bit better than it is right now, it can be a hugely uplifting event.

> Expect A Miracle

Since the release of the book and the website www.expectamiracle.com four years ago, I have witnessed an increase in positive energy from people I have been communicating with.

The generation of a collection of inspiring stories on the website by people from our global 'miracle community' is a joy to witness. The sharing of these heartfelt stories and the lessons in life that people have experienced has enhanced the lives of so many.

I welcome you to join me in this project of spreading the Expect A Miracle message around the world.

By posting a story on www.expectamiracle.com, you give others you have never met a good dose of positivity and encouragement.

Dr John Hinwood

1

MIRACLES OF ATTITUDE

"You see things; and you say, Why? But I dream things that never were; and I say, Why not?"

George Bernard Shaw

Expect A Miracle …
(it is more than a simple card trick)

When you see him do it, you are tempted to believe that Dr John is the reason that the magic happens. You think that it's not so much <u>what</u> he's doing with the cards that creates the magic, but <u>who</u> he is and the way <u>he</u> does it.

And you would be right. But you would also be wrong. It is because of Dr John that so much of it happens – but you don't have to be him to do it. He doesn't ask that you give it a go or tell you that you should try it. In fact, most of his power comes from the fact that he expects nothing from you at all. It is what he expects <u>for</u> you that holds the key. He will tell you (if you ask) that he has done it over 88,000 times – but don't start thinking that it is difficult to do and that you have to practice it over and over and over to get the same sort of result he does. You don't. It is so easy to learn that there isn't really anything much to teach. Just watch Dr John do it a couple of times and before you know it, you will be able to do it yourself.

I know that to be true because I did it and got the same response when I wasn't even expecting a result, and that, dear reader, might just be the key to it all! We were fixing up the bill at the end of a recent catch-up at a local Italian cafe. The waiter serving behind the counter handed Dr John back his validated parking ticket and apologized for the delay as they changed the paper in the EFTPOS terminal. Dr John thanked him and reached into his wallet. Leaning over the counter he said, "Here, this is for you," and he gave the waiter this card:

> **Expect A Miracle**

The waiter looked at the front. Then he turned it over, as everyone who receives one does, to find that there was nothing on the back. No name. No phone number. No website. Nothing. Then, as everyone who receives one does, he looked at Dr John with a sort of confused smile.

Every part of Dr John smiled back as he said, "It's for you. Expect a miracle and I know that you will find one." Magic! Twenty minutes later, I am back in my office and a colleague notices the copy of Dr John's book on my desk with one of his magic cards sticking out in anticipation of being used as a bookmark. I explain to her that he is a friend and we have just caught up over lunch. I say, "Here, let me give you one of his cards..." She looks at the front. Then she turns it over, as everyone who receives one does to find that there is nothing on the back. No name. No phone number. No website. Nothing.

Then, as everyone who receives one does, she looks at me with a sort of confused smile and says, "This isn't a business card?" "No", I say," it's for you, Expect A Miracle" And then it happened.

Like the waiter, there was a visible change in her that went beyond just the physical. It seemed like her whole being let out a huge sigh of relief and relaxed just for a moment. The waiter had responded in much the same way before he caught his breath and reached over the counter to shake Dr John's hand and thank him for his gift.

My colleague thanked me and smiled. She told me that she was facing a number of important decisions at the moment and that a miracle was just what she needed. Now maybe she will get the miracle she is looking for and maybe she won't. As Dr John will tell you, what is important is not having an expectation that a particular miracle will occur, but rather holding a sense of positive expectancy that miracles can be found just about anywhere you look.

And he is right. The miraculous can be found in the most normal of situations if only you have eyes to see it.

Dr Paul Marshall

Australia

> *Logic will get you from A to B, imagination will take you everywhere.*
>
> — Albert Einstein

The Card That Can Put a Twinkle in Anyone's Eye

I remember very clearly the first time I received an "Expect A Miracle" card. I was teaching a week-long seminar about *creating wealth and abundance* in Scotland in a small town called St Andrews. Someone walked up to me during the first day and handed me a card. "Expect A Miracle" was all it said – that's it, no info, no name. And, I loved it. About two days into the program, I was sitting on the stage casually answering some questions and when I tried to get up I couldn't... I described it as my knees just forgot how to work.

My face might have given a clue as to there being a problem, because next thing I knew, the man who'd given me the first card, Dr Clinton McCauley was at my side. Clint is a Chiropractor and "miraculously" was there to remind my knees how to work and also sort out the problem that was causing their "forgetfulness". I asked him about the cards and he told me a story about Dr John Hinwood and Dr Judy Hinwood and the miracles they had influenced in Clinton's life and work including the story of how he'd received his first and many more cards from them; then we went on with the seminar. I silently tucked away the thought that one day I would like to meet these two makers of miracles.

Years later I was teaching a different seminar in

Adelaide, Australia. Clinton was again a participant at this event all about the power of symbols and patterns in our lives and businesses. He handed me a book by Dr John Hinwood signed on the inside cover with notes of thanks from a number of people including John. Clinton had passed on some of my coaching models to a group of people where John was present and he had sent an inscribed copy of his book as a token of thanks. There was also a template in the back for the "Expect A Miracle" cards. I was very thankful and appreciative of the gesture and read the book that night. I loved the idea of joining in the giving away of the cards to people and the difference that could make in their lives.

Four days later I received delivery of my first shipment of cards. Since then, every student, participant, client and customer of mine has received cards. The stories I've heard back and have had happen to me and my family have been amazing and yet... expected, in some way. One was the woman who missed her flight and was anxious and worried till she stumbled upon one of "the cards" in her purse and then smiled calmly and waited. She was then able to get on an even better flight giving her time to rest at the airport, connect with friends and then get a better seat and arrival time. A man who had lost critically important documents for his business was busy tearing his office and house apart to find them. He received a copy of one of my books that he'd ordered and in it, of course, was one of "the cards". He told me he looked at the card that stopped him in his tracks, as he told me later, up to that point he was just been expecting not to find his papers. He changed his thoughts to the miracle of finding them and sure enough did... in the very next place he looked, there they were.

Another story was about a person who really wanted to attend a brand new event I was running and kept one of "the cards" on the bedroom mirror, the bathroom mirror, the computer screen and the steering wheel. Within two weeks, the money had arrived, as well as the time off to allow attendance at the course.

These special miracles and so many others are wonderful, brilliant experiences. The ones I truly love though are the magnificent miracles of every day. I realised the power of this type of miracle working in seminar rooms. As a speaker and trainer, I get to see the amazing job a seminar support Team does in bringing it all together. I started leaving the cards resting on computer keyboards, next to cups of tea or propped up on other pieces of equipment for the Team to find as a surprise. At first they didn't know I was doing it and I would watch for them to find the card.

Let me explain something about the seminar world. These support people work in very high pressure, fast paced environments that can lead to the creating of stress while they do their best

Miracles of Attitude

to serve the trainers and participants. When they would find this card, the looks on faces were fantastic. First there is a look of surprise (*what's this someone's left behind*) then there is an expression of curiosity (*oh, maybe this is a message for me...hmmm*) followed almost immediately by a breath out and then wry smile (*all right, I will then!*) and that's when I knew I'd got them. They were now expecting and sure enough they looked up from the card with new eyes already seeing the world differently.

Many of the people I leave these little surprises for now know they're from me and after they make their silent "all right I will then" declaration they usually look over at me with a knowing smile. I love that. I know they are heading for their own miracles. There's a twinkle in their eye that is unmistakeable.

It's the same twinkle I saw in both John's and Judy's eyes when I was able to meet them a little while after I received John's book as a gift. I have since enjoyed many miracle filled conversations, stories, encounters and sprinkle and sparkle filled cards and continue to do so to this day. Last time I asked John how many cards he'd personally passed on to people in the world... the answer was over 90,000.

I've got a way to go to catch up to that one. I imagine though when I think about those numbers, those cards and all the cards given by people like me who have been influenced by

John. I think of the magnificent, miraculous every-days that flow from each card that can put a twinkle in anyone's eye.

Duane Alley

Australia

> *The first responsibility of a leader is to define reality, the last is to say 'thank you'. In between the two, the leader must become a servant.*
>
> *Max de Pree*

A State Of Expectancy

I am Eric Pearl, and I teach Reconnective Healing around the world. I have a book called *The Reconnection*, which has been published in 27 languages. We do seminars around the globe and we work with John Hinwood in helping healing practitioners learn how to set up and develop healing practices of their own.

One of the things we love is John's Expect A Miracle card. It is different today. When I say it is different, I mean the world is different. If you had received an Expect A Miracle card twenty-five or thirty years ago, you would have thought, "What kind of 'kook' is this person?"

Today, we are recognizing the more subtle energy and consciousness in the world. And what we find, when you hand someone a card that says Expect A Miracle, is that people tend to expect a miracle. It opens them up to a state of expectancy, which is entirely different from one of expectation.

When people come in with expectations of what should happen, what shouldn't happen, how it should happen, what it should smell like, look like, and taste like to the degree that their expectations are met, they might accept the healing only to the degree that their expectations do not appear to be met, or they may very well choose not to accept the healing.

However, when people come in a state of expectancy, there is nothing that needs to be met in the way of certain details. Their state of expectancy is wide open. A childlike state is something that is wide open and allows the gifts of the universe to flow through. As the gifts of the universe are flowing through, the ones that are most perfect for that person are the ones they accept and receive.

The miracle is what they receive.

Dr Eric Pearl

USA

> *You have to move up to another level of thinking, which is true for me and everybody else. Everybody has to learn to think differently, bigger, to be open to possibilities.*
>
> — Oprah Winfrey

It's The Miracle Put Inside The Card

It is Wednesday, 25 June 2008 and I would like to thank you very much for Monday's seminar. It was great and it has completely changed my view of doing my work!

Today I have returned to Prague from Hamburg and within two hours of arriving home I had given away all the "miracle" cards I had received from you. I just had to send them further. It's not just any card, "it's the miracle put inside the card!"

I'm thinking of printing more of these cards. Not because I would be crazy like you, but because Czech people often have dour faces and have forgotten what it is to smile.

Well you wouldn't believe it, but after I got used to the people at the conference, Czech faces seem to me, like professional boxers after having gone ten rounds.

When I gave your card to a person and said 'I got this message from John', they were laughing! Every time! I am laughing! Every time!

Thank you for your inspiration and thank you for bringing smiles into Prague!

Tomas Bouda

Czechoslovakia

> *Miracles in life happen when you are prepared to go to the edge and do what you know is necessary.*
>
> *You may appear crazy to others sometimes, just know deep down, you are not stupid.*
>
> — *Dr John Hinwood*

Is There A Miracle Waiting For You Around The Corner?

I remember years ago, I think the year was 1994. I was in my chiropractic practice taking care of my patients, as I do every single afternoon.

One day we hear a very loud bang and screech in the parking lot. Literally like: bang, bang, bang, and all of a sudden a mighty screech. An old lady had lost control of her car and she hit three cars in the parking lot, got turned towards our office and accidentally stepped on the gas instead of the brake and drove through the centre of my office at 40 mph.

Well, obviously we freaked out. The damage was everywhere. But the damage was more than just the debris of the office. She literally hit several patients, and thank God nobody was killed.

That is one of the miracles, that nobody was killed.

What continued after that was interesting. I went into a "Poor, poor, pitiful me. Why did this happen to me? Here I am serving patients, I have a great practice with tremendous healing chiropractic care, serving my community. God why did you do this to me? Why did you have to make me suffer like this? Why am I dealing with the lawsuit now?" and all the things that were happening as a result of this tragedy.

Well, wouldn't you know it, for the last two years prior to the accident I had been thinking of moving into a new space right around the corner from my house. I had several young children. I wasn't seeing them nearly as much as I really wanted to see them because I was driving 30 minutes to and from work every day.

Well, we got everything sorted out in the office. And I said, "You know what, maybe this is a message, maybe there is a miracle here", and so I opened myself up, I got out of my victim state of mind and the whole poor, poor pitiful me, and I just decided to drive into a shopping centre which is 1.8 miles from my house, where I really, really wanted to practice, but there hadn't been a space available for the last five years the size I wanted.

Wouldn't you know it, one week later I drove into the shopping centre again, and the exact space, and the exact size that I wanted opened up within 7 days. I was open to receive a miracle... and here it was ready for me to say... yes, thank you!!!

So the morale of that story for me was in being open to receive and then expecting a miracle. I think we should all expect miracles every day. If you don't expect them now, maybe a car comes driving through your office or your house or your space to wake you up to the fact that there's a miracle waiting for you right around the corner.

Dr Eric Plasker

USA

> *Out of difficulties grow miracles.*
>
> Jean de la Bryer

Expecting Good and Good is Happening

After becoming familiar with your book You Can Expect A Miracle... The Book To Change Your Life while on holiday in Thailand, I started noticing all the small daily occurrences of miracles happening in my life.

I began to open the weekly management meetings at our college, *Reidman College for Complementary and Integrative Medicine*, here in Israel, with the management team sharing about the miracles in our lives before starting into the business of things and ending the meetings with each one placing an intention for the week.

The relationships among the members have been becoming warmer and more caring with the sharing, the meetings more joyous and less heavy.

We all now have the positive expectation of good things to come, and this in itself is really a miracle. We are expecting good and good is happening.

Thanks for creating the *Expect A Miracle* concept and *Expect A Miracle School*. We are looking forward to participating more fully with it.

Sally Reidman
Israel

> *Some people spread happiness wherever they go, some people spread happiness when they go.*
>
> Oscar Wilde

2

MIRACLES OF COURAGE

Nothing can withstand the power of the human will if it is willing to stake its very existence to the extent of its purpose.

— Benjamin Disraeli

Expect A Miracle Lou

I felt I needed to email you Dr John to let you know that today while wandering around Tweed City looking in the book store I came across this familiar face and name ... yours! I had to have a giggle ... "Gee I know him," I thought. So of course I had to buy your book.

I would like to share with you my experience of *Expect A Miracle*.

On the 14th June last year, my beautiful soul partner of ten years, Eddie, committed suicide here at home. For me and the boys, Josh and Jordy, this was a total shock, because we never saw any signs that Eddie was depressed, let alone suicidal.

Over the weeks after Eddie's passing, I had so much support from many friends and family. I was amazed at how much people really cared for me, the boys, and our darling Eddie.

I received many beautiful cards with lovely caring words, and then one day I got this particular card. On opening it, before I could even see who it was from, there was this white card with big blue writing saying *EXPECT A MIRACLE!* Expect a miracle I thought ... my miracle would be for Eddie to walk up the driveway right now!

On reading the card that was written with so much compassion and love, I found that it was from your friend Berni Ireland. I laughed ... "Typical of Berni," I thought, "and isn't that just what I need?"

I took the *Expect A Miracle* card and placed it in a photo frame that has a picture of Eddie and me that sits in our bedroom. Every night now, before I go to bed, I look at the photo and say, *Expect A Miracle Lou*, and every morning when I wake up, this is the first thing I see.

Well, miracles have come my way, John; I am surviving the most tragic, traumatic thing that has ever happened to me in my life. I am working, looking after my boys, and living my life, something that I didn't think I would ever be able to do without my Eddie. In my deepest, darkest times of emotional despair, I look up and I see our photo of us together and read *Expect A Miracle* ... and I will continue to do so.

I bought your book today and I have finished it already. Thanks, John. It's just what I needed. I am going to recommend it to a support group I belong to. I think it can help many people in shifting their minds. I hope you and Judy and your children are well; my love to you both.

Louise Monaghan

Australia

> *Pain nourishes courage. You can't be brave if you've only had wonderful things happen to you.*
>
> — Mary Tyler Moore

Jumping Off the Story Bridge

One day when I was doing my Nutrimetics calls on my clients, on the spur of the moment I decided to call on my Brownie Guide leader, which I rarely did.

She was all dressed up ready to go somewhere, but stopped and talked. I was always promoting my vitamins, and I really presented very well what vitamin B did for you when you are really uptight. I had first-hand experience, as I had used them before the skiing nationals when I was extremely uptight, and I could share my personal story.

She bought some vitamins, and I happily went on my way.

Months later, one day she said to me, "Remember the day you called on me and sold me the vitamin Bs?" I said, "Yes," starting to think that she may have had a problem with them.

Then she told me that when I had made my surprise call that day, she had just been going out the door to go and jump off the Story Bridge in downtown Brisbane and commit suicide. She told me that the chat we'd had that day had been her life-saver.

She went on to say that some things we talked about and shared that day, and my positive attitude, had saved her life. She thanked me from the bottom of her heart, and said that since then, her dramas had sorted themselves out.

Never underestimate the power of your intuition, as my spur of the moment call that day produced the miracle of a saved life, and allowed a new life to be born in that person.

Eloise Anderson

Australia

> *A happy person is not a person in a certain set of circumstances, but rather a person with a certain set of attitudes.*
>
> *Hugh Downs*

I 'Hit the Wall' Six Times In My Life

Understanding that miracles happen on a regular occurrence in our lives is something I take for granted. I have had many 'angels' come into my life, support me through the tough times, and often just disappear or stay close by as close friends. I now see the miracles daily and say thank you for such wonderful blessings that support the changes in my world.

I have hit the wall six times in my life; from urgent and drastic surgeries, a severed limb and fractures, experiencing life in a wheel chair, suffering deep depression, auto immune diseases, and finally the most challenging time was losing my short term memory for eighteen months.

I am going to talk about the memory loss part of my journey, which crept up on me over a period of time in the early 2000's. The final crash came when the stress of working for someone who handed over the reins of his business to me, because he wasn't prepared to take on the responsibility that was necessary. I became the rescuer again, a repeated pattern which I have taken on many times during my life.

For me, I learnt, later of course, that is was not my business to do what I did in the name of 'rescuing his business'. It was time for him to take personal responsibility. After some time and much effort, through incredible obstacles which would have had any sane individual saying 'enough is enough', I started to crack gradually, and then experienced a total blow out. Eventually I couldn't remember the basic things I needed to remember.

It was agreed that I wasn't functioning at my best and that I needed to take some time out. I was in a state of shock as my mind was not doing what it needed to do to function correctly. I was diagnosed initially as suffering depression, stress and chronic fatigue. I was yet to find out the cause of what was happening, which will unfold as I tell my story.

By this time I was really loosing myself and my life ... or so it seemed.

I had a presentation talk to give to a group of business people and it was during this talk that I realised I had lost the plot! I could not remember what I was talking about or keep my train of thought. For someone who had always prided themselves on a good memory, and people commented frequently on the fact that it was exceptional, it was devastating. I had built my network as a result of my memory and relationship building.

Fortunately, I have been blessed to have a doctor who is always prepared to look outside the box, so to speak, and he is my number one miracle. Without him, I would not be alive today.

Thank you Dr Frank.

My number two miracle happened as I was fortunate to afford to be able do a Ten Day Detox Retreat programme at Living Valley Springs at Kin Kin. The day I was leaving I had some time with Gary Martin, who owned the centre, as he had been away during my retreat. He asked me to open my mouth.

Voila!! I was told, I had an electrical mine field in my mouth. It appeared that there were five different heavy metals in my mouth and as I was informed, anyone who has done any chemistry should know that you do not mix heavy metals. It appears that dentists in their wisdom had created this mine field. It was no wonder my memory had gone. Thank you Gary.

He made a phone call there and then to Dr Eric Davis, and my number three miracle happened. Eric is Australia's best qualified dentist on heavy metal removal. Usually there is a twelve month wait to see him, and knowing that he was unable to work with me, he said as a favour he would see me for a check-up a few days later. When I had the check-up, this wonderful man said that he would not let anyone else touch me owing to the fact that it could be too dangerous. Within days I was having all sorts of tests to see what was happening, as it was obvious that I was going to need all the heavy metal removed along with a root canal treatment. This was going to take some time. In fact, it was six months before it was safe to actually start any removal of metal from my mouth. I was put onto a nutritional protocol, with a Vitamin C drip at every session, which continued for the length of the whole process to help alleviate the stress and shock that was happening in my body. It appeared that I had mercury and lead poisoning. It was going to be a painstaking time ahead. Thank you Eric.

During this time my number four miracle came through my sister, suggesting that I get my doctor to run some particular tests as a result of symptoms I had. Fortunately, he was happy to run these unusual tests, which came back with results that not only surprised him but me too. I was diagnosed with three auto-immune diseases for starters. Without him I would not be here today to tell this story, as his treatment was very much different from the usual treatments given. So different, that my disability insurance wiped me after six months as I would not use their recommended treatments. Dr Frank has become, over thirty years, a wonderful friend and confidant.

By this time my memory was so bad that I didn't know what was happening in my life. My health was too bad to be doing any heavy metal removal, as I was still working on getting well enough for this to happen.

My fifth miracle happened when my close friend Linda arrived to see me from the Gold Coast. It was late morning and I was sitting in my kitchen still in night clothes trying to fill in a form for my insurance company. When she realised that I didn't remember basically my name or where I lived, she made the decision to come and live with me. This meant leaving her marriage and moving back to Brisbane. She and Ben, her beautiful German shepherd dog, arrived and stayed for nearly a year. She always jokes that she is not sure who was totally insane at the end of it all. Without her along with all the therapy we did on a daily basis, I would not have come through that time of deep depression. She tells me that I sat with my back to the world a lot of the time, like a Nun, closing off. I started scrap booking and spent hours just playing with photos of my life trying to recall and put everything into perspective. Thank you Linda for the blessings you gave me.

Whilst I was going through the removal process my sixth miracle came in the form of another friend, a medical doctor, who worked spiritually and started seeing me weekly, doing some counselling and giving me a Vitamin B drip weekly saying, when I could jump off the table she would stop the treatments. This continued on for about six months until I had most of my energy levels back. This was a time of just not wanting to live any longer and not being able to see a light at the end of a very deep tunnel. Thank you Kathy for your support and friendship during this time.

Dr John Hinwood

Miracle number seven happened with some incredible friends who rallied around, visited and just did their best to keep me moving forward. Without their incredible support, love and care I do not believe I would have moved forward. I started to work again and realise that there was a life to live. Thank you to all those who supported me through this time of sheer confusion!

Now, ten years on, I have discovered another miracle ... 'earthing'. My blood tests show the SLE (Lupus) is no longer there; the Rheumatoid Arthritis has gone; my diabetes has gone to being almost not detectable; my blood pressure has gone to 100/60; I sleep better and need much less sleep than I have ever needed. Waking refreshed early and ready to go; I am in total flow and balanced for the first time in my life. So many other changes came with my work moving forward as it never had before, a better bank balance and beautiful relationships to top it off.

I am blessed ... I see every day as a blessing and a miracle and know that I do not need to 'hit that wall' ever again!

Jennie Gorman

Australia

> *Yes, I have doubted, I have wandered off the path. I have been lost. But I have always returned. It is beyond the logic I seek. It is intuitive... an intrinsic, built-in sense of direction. I seem to find my way home. My faith has wavered but has saved me.*
>
> *— Helen Hayes*

3

MIRACLES OF FAMILY

My mother has always been unhappy with what I do. She would much rather I do something nicer, like be a bricklayer.

Mick Jagger

Dr John Hinwood

Expecting My Miracle Baby

It had taken six years for my husband to talk me into having another baby, as my first experience of child birth had been a 30 hour nightmare. So when Christopher and I started trying it was with a few nerves that I waited each month to see if 'it had worked yet'. After nine months, nothing was happening, but as I lay on a table during a visit to an energy healer, I mentioned the challenge we were having and he 'waved his hands over my abdomen in just the right way' and bam, I was pregnant a few weeks later.

Telling Christopher was exciting, as I waited until his return from a short trip away to do the proper test, but knew firmly in my heart that it was so. Alas, the stick indicated a negative, not a positive result. That same week, he got sick. In fact, he was dangerously ill, though we didn't know it at the time. I was still sure I was pregnant too, and despite all the other things going on with him being taken into hospital for tests, I re-did my own test – still the stick was telling me I wasn't pregnant, and the doctors were finding no answers to what was going on with Christopher either. They sent him home with a prescription for some paracetemol; he went home to bed, and I went to the pharmacist to fill the prescription.

I of course picked up yet another pregnancy test, and went home gave him some panadol, and took the test yet again. STILL nothing.

We both headed for the doctors surgery a few days later, and while Christopher had his blood taken and checked again, I had mine checked for pregnancy – finally my pregnancy was confirmed. Now all we had to do was get my husband back on his feet and life would be wonderful!

A few days later, he was taken by ambulance into hospital, where 2 days later he was put into ICU in an induced coma. He rallied and was awake again nine long days later, and we joyfully talked about many things, ending the conversation with "I love you's" fully expecting he was now on the mend. That was the last time I saw him awake and 'well' – he died unexpectedly a few days later.

We announced my pregnancy at his funeral – and as 'Peanut' was due on the 1st April and Chris was very well known as a practical joker, a few people did wonder if this was a bad taste joke.

As I grieved, I grew, and had to face giving birth again, this time without my lovely husband beside me. *I simply could not bear the idea of it,* and finally managed to convince the doctor to send me to an Obstetrician (instead of registering me with a midwife), who I then *begged* to give me an elective caesarean section. He finally said that I was healthy and saw no good reason to do this, but if I went past the 1st April, he would. Well I kept my legs crossed, and waited, and waited, and then finally on the 3rd April turned up ready for my delivery.

It's also relevant to note that during my entire pregnancy I somehow avoided having any scans or regular checkups, and was glowingly healthy. There was no reason for any concern – I just didn't want to go through a long labour without Christopher. BUT, on the operating table, the Obstetrician announced with relief – "Well Maria, that was a very lucky call, your baby had the cord wrapped around his neck *and* it was knotted. A natural delivery would have been 'very difficult' indeed". What an understatement!

During that final conversation with his father, we both picked only one name for him or her – Alex. My little miracle baby is now 14 years old, and an absolute joy - and very much like his father too.

Maria Carlton

New Zealand

Miracles occur naturally as expressions of love. The real miracle is the love that inspires them. In this sense everything that comes from love is a miracle.

Marianne Williamson

The Power of Family

One of my miracle stories is about my family. For a long time I was moved around with my family, as my dad was in the military. Although I depended on them, I always found my friends to be more my family.

At twenty-one years of age I became pregnant and had a son, who is now almost five. I had dropped out of school, was working in a bar, and had no direction in my life. I felt that when I became pregnant my family would not be supportive, but in fact they were the opposite.

My two brothers were very supportive and became very excited uncles, my mom told me to come back home, and my Dad told me to go back to school. So at twenty-one, I was working full-time, and ten days after I quit my job, I gave birth to my son, and three months later I went back to school.

With the support of my family, I lived at my mother's house for three years. I raised my son with my mother's support. She was like a stand-in dad, and my dad would help me at nights.

When I finished my degree, I discovered many of my other passions, along with my son; health, exercise and just being with my family, and during the last six years I have begun to realize the power of family. It has helped me to shape my son, and helped him understand the power of family, and has also helped me bring my partner into our lives.

There has been a lot going on in my family, where no one turns their back and walks away, but stands alongside each other. It's something that you learn as you grow up and move around a lot, but you take it for granted. Having my own son and starting my own family, I have learned the hard way, and it has really opened my eyes. To me, that is a miracle, because some people go their whole lives without knowing their family.

I truly know my family, and the love my family has for me, and the love I have for my family, my son and my partner; that is my miracle story.

Heather Fulwider

USA

> *Sometimes letting it go is an act of far greater power than defending or hanging on.*
> — Eckhart Tolle

Expect A Miracle is a Great Message

I'm Simon Austin of Winchester Chiropractic Clinic, and I've been working in England since 1997.

I first met John in Australia in 1993, and we touched base again at one of his practice management seminars at Heathrow in London in1997. At the end of the seminar, he mentioned the Expect A Miracle cards that he had been handing out for over twenty years. John gave me this card at that seminar.

I took the card home, and that evening my wife told me that we were expecting our second child. If there is a miracle in life, it has a little bit to do with birth. I am quite analytical, and into science and diagnoses, but I would like to believe there are miracles out there. On that occasion, John showed me I should expect miracles, and indeed my little boy George, who has just turned two, is a miracle.

So thank you, John. Expect A Miracle is a great message.
Dr Simon Austin

England

Strategic words have vibrations that delight.

Oscar Wilde

Dr John Hinwood

My Expect A Miracle Card Brings Good Luck

I do not class myself as an unlucky person, however I was finding things were not going my way lately. I went to visit my grandson who was telling me about the Expect A Miracle website and the little white cards known as "Expect A Miracle" cards.

He explained to me how to make them and that you needed a printer to do this. At 80 I was thinking about neither having a computer nor a printer. The next thing you know he pulled two little white cards out of his pocket and as he passed them to me said, Nan, "Expect A Miracle".

I thanked him for the cards and put them in my wallet knowing I had a long drive to my daughters the next week. I thought I would give the second card to her as she had been down on her luck lately.

One week later, I set out to my daughter's house in Bindah which was a long drive of nearly three hours on bush roads. As I was driving, I heard a strange sound and thought I may have an issue with my tyre. As I had just had everything checked and serviced with the car, I was quite shocked at this.

I pulled the car over and checked the tyre; however I could see nothing wrong with it. I continued on my travels happy that the annoying sound had stopped. About an hour later, I realised I only had fifty kilometres to go before I arrived at my daughter's house.

I had slowed down as I was driving through a small country town that was a 50km zone. There was a large bang! I pulled the car over and realised I was in front of a mechanics shop. I remember thinking, "oh that's lucky". On getting out of the car I walked around to the front and I looked at my tyre. It was a horrible sight to see that my tyre had exploded, right there in front of a mechanics shop.

The mechanic came out to see what was wrong. I asked him to please fix it, which he did. He told me how I was very lucky that if it had exploded on the country road half an hour back, I could have been seriously injured. I just remember thinking "Expect A Miracle".

When I went back to my grandson's house I asked him for more Expect A Miracle cards and now always keep one handy.

Ann Napper

Australia

> *Miracles happen every day, change your perception of what a miracle is and you will see them all around you.*
>
> *Jon Bon Jovi*

My Miracle Daughter

This miracle story involves my ten year old daughter.

When she was seven weeks old when she was diagnosed with meningitis and it was a very serious situation and she was so very young and new. The doctors told us she probably would not make it through.

We hit the floor with our knees and started praying, we thought positive and stayed up with her four days straight. It was amazing, a miraculous recovery because what the doctors told us what would happen, did not happen.

In fact, Hannah is a very exciting, vibrant young lady today. I often make jokes, that I prayed for her when she was sick and asked the Lord to give her extra strength to get through it.

Hannah has a lot of energy, she loves to help people, she is a servant at heart, she is exciting and I joke that God gave her an over-dose of energy and it has carried on throughout her life.

I expect great things from this young lady.

Shawn Bean

USA

> *What the mind of man can conceive and believe, it can achieve.*
>
> — Napoleon Hill

4

MIRACLES OF FREEDOM

Freedom is not worth having if it does not include the freedom to make mistakes.

Mahatma Ghandi

Dr John Hinwood

It Was an Unexpected Miracle

John, you may like to hear about a couple of miracles that have come from your Expect A Miracle cards. I have given them out all around town since buying a pack from you when you presented your keynote, Creating Miracles in Your Business at the Bellingen Chamber of Commerce. I've given them to strangers, shopkeepers and friends.

A week or so ago, I walked into my local butcher's shop and he started quizzing me. I am not their best customer, as I mostly only buy meat for my dog.

I had felt moved to give him a card without knowing he had a problem. It turns out he had Bell's Palsy, which affected one side of his face much like a stroke, and usually takes nine months to settle down. He was better in three weeks!

It was the talk of the butchery the next time I went in, and the owner felt a bit left out; he wanted a card too. He hadn't been there the day I gave the initial card out, so I gave him one.

For me, it was an unexpected miracle ... not what I had been thinking about at all, but something I needed now.

Out of the blue, I was gifted two tightly packed truckloads of firewood from someone I hardly know that was worth more than $300!

Thanks for reminding us to expect miracles in our lives.

Susan Haworth
Australia

> *People need to believe they are worthy of a miracle, because that thought alone can change a life.*
>
> *Dr John Hinwood*

That Card Made Her Day

Hey John,

Barb was at a stop light the other day in downtown Guam near where we live, and she happened to glance at a car ahead of her. She caught a vision of an Expect A Miracle card that was taped to the back of a sun visor. We've been handing them out for a while now, so it is nice to "bump" into them around the island. Barb was so happy to see it; that card made her day.

Take care.

Rob Gregory

Guam

The soul never thinks without a picture.

Aristotle

All The Little Miracles That Surround Me

At Expect A Miracle School on Saturday you asked us to write about one of the miracles in our lives. I have experienced so many miracles that it was a joy on Saturday to remind myself to celebrate and acknowledge all the little miracles that surround me.

One of the miracles in my life is all of the beautiful people who have had an impact on my life - family, friends, work colleagues and acquaintances. Many years ago I was given a "Circle of Friends" candle holder. I started to write on the base all the people I had gratitude for - people who had impacted my life and who I cared about.

My personal miracle is that the base is now almost completely full. Judy and John Hinwood are on there. Thank you for being in my life. You are both an inspiration and your enthusiasm; love and generosity are beautiful gifts you share with the world. THANK YOU.

Love and Hugs,

Cathy Duncan

Australia

> *Miracles, in the sense of phenomena we cannot explain, surround us on every hand: life itself is the miracle of miracles.*
>
> George Bernard Shaw

5

MIRACLES OF HEALTH & HEALING

It is a funny thing about life; if you refuse to accept anything but the best, you very often get it.

W. Somerset Maugham

Dr John Hinwood

How to Make Lemonade... First You Need Some Lemons

In July 2007 I collapsed suddenly while writing a report in my newly built chiropractic office in Bendigo, Victoria. I can clearly remember what I was doing up to the moment of my collapse, and how good I felt as I was nearing completion of the task at hand.

BANG!!!! Was all I heard. Like a shotgun blast inside my head. Then the darkness imploded to a pinhole of light, just like turning off a television.

I awoke on the floor of my office, on the other side of my chiropractic table from where I had been sitting at the computer, with two paramedics attending me.

There were three women standing quietly against the far wall. One was my wife Joanne, the other my chiropractic assistant Lisa, and the final lady was my local colleague, chiropractic neurologist Dr Helen Sexton.

The paramedics' questions came thick and fast...

"Can you tell me your name?"

"Who is the Prime Minister of Australia?"

"What day is it?"

"How many children do you have?"

In my awakening state, I correctly answered "four children" to the last question, and there was muffled laughter from the ladies. A few minutes earlier apparently I had muttered "Children? What children?"

My left cheek, lip, and tongue felt like I had been chewing on a cheese grater; the taste of blood was salty and raw.

Apparently I'd had a grand-mal seizure, where my whole torso had gone into violent extension, and I'd lurched backwards at full power straight over the top of the chiropractic table. My whole left side was thumping super-fast while I fitted on the floor. I bit down ferociously with my molars on my tongue and cheek.

The paramedics insisted I lie down on a stretcher, even though I felt quite capable of getting up and about, if not a bit dazed. They bundled me into the ambulance for the start of an interesting trip, which was a dizzying rollercoaster of negatives and positives for the next two years, and from which we are only just starting to fully recover from financially, physically, and emotionally six years down the track.

Initially I was diagnosed with a fairly lethal type of brain tumour with a grim prognosis. This was called a mixed anaplastic oligoastrocytoma, a tumour that sent out a 'root system' like a weed would, all through my brain. This condition had a median survival time of eighteen months. An exploratory craniotomy confirmed it was inoperable, but treatable with chemotherapy and radiation therapy. The tumour remained stable for quite some time.

A year later it took off again, changing rapidly to the most lethal of all brain tumours; a grade four glioblastoma multiforme. Emergency neurosurgery while I was fully conscious managed to skillfully remove the central core of the tumour, but the specialists still expected that I would last only a few months. In fact, Zurich Insurance paid me out on my life insurance within six weeks of receiving the claim form signed by the oncologist and the neurosurgeon. Apparently in the small print of my insurance contract there was a clause covering terminal disease conditions.

I wrote a letter to the Zurich insurance assessor for processing my claim, with a photo of my wife and I and our five young children letting him know how much it meant to all of us. I received a reply a week or so later to say they were delighted to help out, and that they very rarely received letters from claimants or their families. Apparently my letter and our family photo were placed in their board room as a "reason why we do what we do".

The six figure pay out sum took massive stress off us financially, but after the collapse of my little real-estate portfolio and paying out all the costs that had accrued after my collapse, there was

Miracles of Health & Healing

not enough left to do any serious investing again. I didn't want to let my kids remember me as some ailing guy with a drip in his arm, so I refused an offer of a powerful chemotherapy agent.

Not knowing at that stage quite what turn to take, we took the whole family to New Zealand for Christmas. We toured both islands in a motor home. That was a lot of fun, and we then decided to take the whole family on a round-world trip for fourteen weeks. We hit all the major museums, galleries, castles, and landmarks we could in Europe, went on a Greek Islands cruise, visited Boston, New York, and Colorado, then finished off with a sopell in Fiji. I celebrated the first anniversary of my likely demise by taking a jet ski out past the reef into the big surf, and showing the older kids what their dad used to do.

This early pay out was a miracle for our family. It was an amazing emotional boost to my spirit, to only keep expecting the best possible outcomes.

Nearly five years down the track from the second neurosurgery, not only am I alive and well, but also exercising vigorously most days, and living as if the condition never occurred. How am I so well when statistically I had only a three percent chance of even being alive at this stage? I think it's because I've never allowed myself to worry about it, or admit it has any power in my life. I also have a strong, basic Christian faith and a loving family.

Dr John Hinwood

I won't deny that I went through some very tough and upsetting times in all of this, but as far as I could I have always concentrated on my best possible outcome. If you want to get better from a brain disease, keep acting the way you want to end up; in other words- keep 'faking' and 'faithing' till you get there. It worked for me.

After continually awaking every day to find I was fine and still going OK, I became more and more used to the idea I was supposed to be here for some time, despite all the doubters. I had my "little issues" with fatigue and financial stresses, but bit by bit I got back to a more normal life.

I'll share a story with you about how I've tried to turn every possible negative into a positive. The main thing I've found is if you can still laugh, then the cancer entity can't 'win'. Fear and worry are the killers.

One week when I was going OK, nearly a year after my first collapse, I was driven up to the little isolated farm property we had by Australia's mighty Murray River. I hadn't seen the property in all the time I'd been ill. The tenant we somehow acquired when I was away with the fairies in Bendigo was a chain-smoking bachelor with one lung who smelt of car gearbox, old dog, stale sweat, fusty beer, nicotine and musty marijuana. He also had no idea about paying rent or doing the basic maintenance of watering and mowing we asked of him for the modest rental.

He'd held a week-long 'clothing-optional hippy love in fest ' with over two hundred 'invited guests' on the property. The locals never informed us because he'd told them all in the pub that he'd bought the property from us. We'd had the whole Woodstock thing going on; the communal mattress in the middle of the paddock, the bongo drums, and the old iron water-tank stand bodily lifted and moved two hundred metres to the edge of the river for the drummer to sit on top of. It must've resembled the building of the pyramids.

He'd also arranged thirteen stolen Council wheelie rubbish bins in a circle around a large gum tree out of sight of the house and the road, and these were all chained to the tree and each other. The wheels had all been removed just in case someone else decided to steal them off him. The bins were joined at their bases by an ingenious sequence of large PVC pipes and brackets, and filled to varying degrees by sawdust, water, human excrement, and toilet paper. Each lid had a hole cut into it for defecation purposes.

Anyhow, you get the picture. Once I'd seen and heard about what he'd done, I left him a note requesting he vacate immediately, with the promise that if he wasn't gone within two weeks, I'd start moving all of his accumulated junk to the edge of the property to be put into a big dumpster.

Early in the winter, when I was dropped off on the appointed day, he and his mutt were nowhere to be seen, and several of his trucks had gone, but all his accumulated scrap iron and junk still filled a formerly empty large shed. Old fridges, freezers, washing machines, beds; copper pipes, galvanized iron, crappy wires; anything that didn't have a hope in hell of resurrection was hoarded in my shed. Crammed to the edges and overflowing with his treasures.

He'd also let a little paddock right beside the gardens go to seed, and I had no hope of clearing it all up quickly with the tractor and blade because he'd taken my big petrol can and left the battery stone cold dead. The same situation applied to my big ride-on mower; dead battery and no petrol. Luckily the kangaroos and the long dry summer had made long grass a non-issue.

I didn't have a car, and the local mechanic was away for that week, so this presented a bit of a problem. I was preparing the property for sale, but it was unpresentable in the state my tenant had left it in.

It so happened that the major weed that had taken over my little paddock was a very nasty one that bore a remarkable physical and physiological resemblance to my then-nemesis, the oligoastrocytoma. 'Tribulus Terrestris' is a spiteful weed of uncertain origins that is endemic in parts of the Southern Mediterranean, North

Africa, and Asia. Its grotesque multi-spiked seed heads look like the face of Satan, and when they mature they harden and can puncture car tyres. The seeds can lie latent in dry sandy soils for years, and can come to life within a day or so of any decent rain. Bizarrely, the central fleshy tap-root or tuber has been used for centuries as a source of male aphrodisiac tonics.

It has gone by many common names in different countries, including cat's head, devil's eyelashes, devil's thorn, devil's weed, goat head, puncturevine, and in Australia: 'Caltrop' or 'bindii' (pronounced 'bindy-eye').

I had several problems to solve in my time at the property. Any of these problems could have been solved by paying someone a bit of cash to help out. But at that stage, after months of going without any form of income, all reserves were gone, and cash was in short supply.

In the interim I decided that I'd use this opportunity of being totally alone for the month to work physically all day long from dawn to sundown, and sleep with the cycles of nature. Joanne arranged to visit once a week and top up my food supplies. I'd had enough of becoming a flabby, soft, middle-aged convalescent.

I decided to use the lack of tractor as an incentive to exercise hard instead. I've found, nearly always, that the reason NOT to do something is nearly always the same reason TO DO something!

I'd get woken up at dawn by the cacophony of thousands of cockatoos flying overhead, and after preparing a hot cooked breakfast with coffee, I'd get stuck into the work at hand. I prayed a prayer of thanks for the immediate problems all being solved.

The weeds were the first major obstacle to overcome. The second was the disposal of all the wheelie bins with their human manure. The third major problem was the disposal of all the junk in my shed.

With my garden gloves, a good rake, and a sharp spade as my major tools, I set about digging out every single clump of caltrop I saw. This was easy, because I told myself that with each one I plucked out by the long tuber, I was destroying yet another projection of the tumour in my brain. The subconscious mind apparently cannot distinguish between a vividly imagined event and 'reality', so you can see how that whole paddock got cleared up completely within two days.

It is a fact of physiology that one can perform intense exercise without incurring major fatigue as long as the bursts last less than 10 seconds on average. This intense activity, with reasonable recovery intervals, exercises the most powerful muscle fibres we possess, the Type IIB , using an intramuscular fuel called creatine phosphate that keeps replenishing itself when given a suitable recovery. It also produces none of the lactic acid that slightly longer bursts of very intense activity would produce. For this reason it is known as alactic exercise.

I'd very vigorously attack the centre of each large weed clump for the alactic exercise burst, then recover with far easier aerobic activity as I raked the large fronds in to the centre of the clump I'd just attacked.

This constant aerobic recovery/ short alactic power burst activity really woke up my whole body, and by the time I'd plucked all the weeds out and placed the 'tumour fronds' into thirteen large gatherings I'd made around the paddock, I felt as strong as I ever have in my life. I only stopped for a quick lunch of fruit and toast with marmalade, and a cup of tea. I drank rainwater from a bottle I had with me in the paddock.

Each of the thirteen 'wheel-less' 1000 litre wheelie bins was at least half-full of wet sawdust and faeces, and weighed several hundred kilograms apiece. Without my tractor, it would be very difficult to get all of them two hundred metres away, up the slope of the paddock and across to where I was hoping to empty them in a ring where I could rake them over and make them into a very large compost pile to stack beside the cottage gardens.

I cut the chains with the large bolt cutters that

my tenant hadn't stolen, undid the crude plumbing connections, and allowed the stinking liquid in each bin to seep into the sand where it stood. While that slow process was happening, I removed myself from the stench and attacked other parts of the garden with a hacksaw. However, the sawdust in the bins was still absolutely sodden, so I set about dragging these massive weights in very short distances with the resistance of the sand to contend with as well. This was an ideal exercise to build back in some whole-body phasic-muscle core strength. I dragged each wheelie bin to a position beside the removed tumours, and emptied the bin beside it.

Then I raked and shovelled the 'tumours fronds' into the empty bins at each clump, and dragged these much lighter bins to my planned cremation site.

I'd already dragged hundreds of pruned branches from my long-suffering fruit trees to the cremation site, and I gleefully shovelled all my amassed tumour material onto the funeral pyre. The blaze was magnificent, and I stayed patrolling the embers until darkness came.

"Keith! Get to bed- NOW!" said a voice in my head. It had such authority that I did exactly that and lay down just as the aura of a large seizure came, hovered threateningly for some minutes over me, and then went. I'd gone all day without taking my anti-seizure medication, and with only my breakfast and light lunch. Whatever entity

Miracles of Health & Healing

was attacking me certainly hated what I'd just accomplished, but I knew I was being looked after by a far more powerful force.

The next morning, after a very large breakfast, and feeling very happy, I set about the task of gathering up all the drying compost piles back into the wheelie bins. These I then dragged up to my compost heap beside the cottage gardens.

I had asked the dumpster delivery man to leave two of his biggest dumpsters beside my shed full of junk. The dumpsters were massive steel bins I could walk around, each having a thirty cubic metres capacity.

There was a cold thick winter mist creeping up from the creek. The sun was a vague yellow orb I could just make out through the fog. I gazed at my very large shed, and set about heaving and shoving several large ancient electric stoves and refrigerators into one bin. Two men I did not know ranged up from the end of my property and suggested that I'd be far better off ringing up the scrap metal dealer from Rochester, another country town an hour or so away. They told me that all the metal would fetch good money as scrap metal prices at that stage were sky-high. They also said he'd bring his loader with him and do the whole cleanup on-site.

I thanked them warmly, and then they wandered away, but not before they insisted on helping me remove the items I'd just shoved into the big bin. "What good fellows" I thought, then considered how odd it was that two ordinary-looking men I'd never seen before would stroll up on my remote property proffering such good advice, in a winter mist, before most people were out of bed.

I rang the dealer as advised, and he duly came and cleaned out the entire shed of anything with metal in it. He and his work partner had it all done in a couple of hours with his special forklift and various useful tools. He said he'd weigh all the different items back at his depot, and pay me the next week by cheque.

While the men from Rochester were emptying my shed's contents for me, I dragged a large lump of concrete I'd tied to an old thick blanket, up and down the paddock to pick up any stray heads of caltrop thorns from the dust. The blanket I then burnt as well.

I still had the problem of getting rid of thirteen stolen council wheelie bins. I'd been told by an officious council employee that as the ratepayer on the property, I was responsible for the safe disposal of these bins, not the council. He also helpfully informed me that I was personally liable should the Environmental Protection Agency find that I had allowed a portable septic system to be built without permits on my property, which was located in a national park.

I filled all the bins equally with other detritus I found around the property, and then neatly stacked them at the base of the two big dumpsters. These I then covered with enough

Miracles of Health & Healing

loose junk to disguise the whole lot.

A cheque for over thirteen hundred dollars arrived in the mail at home from the scrap metal dealer, and this was enough to pay for the hire of the dumpsters, and give us a much-needed cash injection at the same time.

I'll finish up now as it's getting late in the day and I need to get out on my mountain bike and get my daily hour in. Needless to say I am fit and well, and continue to believe I will be so for a good time yet.

I sincerely hope I've inspired someone out there with strategies for dealing with tough situations.

Miracles in life often come as the result of problem-solving exercises, really. You keep going until you decide you can't solve any more problems.

Dr Keith Livingstone

Australia

> *He who has a WHY can live with almost any HOW.*
>
> *Victor Frankl*

Dr John Hinwood

Postponing Babe's Suicide: The Mind, Body Connection

It is unfathomable but real ... a person's recovery can allow them to feel so alive and human again that they actually think twice about suicide.

No, it is not uncommon in health care to hear patients speak of a pain experience so bad that they think about ending their lives. They could be atheists, Christians, or any number of personal profiles. The common thread is that we are all human, and pain, when unrelenting, drives us to seek an exit.

In my opinion, the mortal sin is not in the taking of one's life so much as never being given an option in regard to the solution to the cause of the problem.

One such man came to see me. He was insular but polite. He confessed to bursts of rage, and had a temper that had earned him Apprehended Violence Orders through the wielding of a baseball bat more than once. And he was not playing ball. It was not even that he did it without cause, because it was often things like clients not paying bills or people being cruel and unreasonable that set him off. But this man, Babe, shall we call him (baseball fans should get the reference to Mr Ruth) had a history of abuse you could only encounter in a nightmare.

The short of it is that Babe's neck was also killing

Miracles of Health & Healing

him. Referred by a naturopath and benefactor, Jack, he came to see me with a downward stare but a sparkle of likeability that has burned to this day.

He got better after we adjusted his neck with a specific chiropractic adjustment, not random manipulation or traction or the like.

Sometime later in his program of care, he confessed that a miracle had occurred, as he had postponed his suicide because he felt so much better. Actually, he has cancelled it, as far as I know.

Dr Joseph Ierano

Australia

Not only must you know what you want, but you must really want what you want, if you are to get what you want.
                                        David McNally

Dr John Hinwood

What You Think About … Comes About

I have a friend who suffered a horrific car crash on December 8, 2008. He was struck by an eighteen-wheeler and suffered a fractured 4th lumbar vertebra, four broken ribs and, most significantly, a fracture of the atlas vertebra.

The atlas is the top bone in the neck, and it houses and protects the brain stem, which is the Grand Central Station of the nervous system.

This man was told that he was lucky to be alive, and that they basically did not know why he was alive, with no spinal cord damage. To cut to the chase, they put him in a rigid neck brace and told him to come back in six weeks. After six weeks, there was no healing and things looked grim. The neurosurgeon explained that his neck was unstable and that there was a fragment of bone sitting on the right vertebral artery, and if he moved his head toward his right shoulder it would sever the artery and he would die instantly. If he moved his head toward his left shoulder, a fragment of bone was sitting on the left side of his brainstem and spinal cord that would be severed, and he would instantly become a tetraplegic. They said he would need to spend six more weeks in the collar, and then undergo surgery to fuse the top two bones in his neck to his skull, a very risky procedure. He really did not want this risky surgery, but the surgeons told him that it was inevitable.

Miracles of Health & Healing

This person, who had been under chiropractic care since the age of four, did not want surgery because he understood the risk involved and the importance of this area of his nervous system.

We had dinner shortly after he received the news, and he asked for my help. I told him he needed to spend ten minutes every day seeing his neck totally healed, and to feel the feelings he would feel if he had just found out his neck was perfectly healed. I put my hands on his neck and visualized the same outcome for him. His eldest daughter committed to doing the exercise as well.

The result at his next check-up showed almost complete healing, which the medical specialists could not explain, and no need for surgery. A true miracle!

So, what do you visualize before, during, and after your adjustment? What do you expect from your chiropractic care? How much time do you spend visualizing how you would like your life to look every day? Remember, *what your mind can conceive and believe, it can achieve*, for that is why we have an innate intelligence that runs our body.

Dr Peter Amlinger

Canada

> *There's a difference between interest and commitment. When you're interested in doing something, you do it only when it's convenient. When you're committed to doing something, you accept no excuses, only results.*
>
> — Kenneth Blanchard

Miracles of Health & Healing

The Clenched Fist

One story that I will never forget was a 70-year old woman who came to see me with neck pain, and when I walked into the examination room to take my history, I noted that she had hearing aids in both ears, and I didn't pay any attention to it. She proceeded to tell me her chief complaint was her neck. It had bothered her for a couple of years. She had some trouble moving it, she had some stiffness, and it made some crackling noises when she moved it around, and she was coming to me to get help for that.

So I proceeded with my examination and took my x-rays, and the next day she came in for the Report of Findings. I explained to her what I thought was wrong with her neck and what it would take to help it. I prescribed a series of adjustments twice a week for about six weeks to start with.

I sat her down in a chair and gave her a cervical chair adjustment. It was to the 6th cervical vertebrae at the base of the neck. It wasn't a great adjustment, didn't make a lot of movement, didn't make a lot of noise. I would love to claim that was a terrific adjustment, but it wasn't my best, so I sent her home and thought nothing of it.

She came back the next day. I walked into the adjusting room and there she was standing with a clenched fist. That was the first thing I noticed, and I got scared. I thought she was going to hit me. I had done something wrong, I instantly thought. However, when I looked up, I saw tears in her eyes and she slowly opened up her hand, and when I looked down at it, there were those two hearing aids.

And she said "Doc, ever since you adjusted my neck, I don't need these any more. I can hear excellently right now for the first time in about eight years". We both cried about that for a while. It was so amazing. It was the first time I had ever had a hearing improvement in a patient. I had heard it happen to other chiropractors (of course that is how chiropractic got started, by the healing of a deaf man by the name of Harvey Lillard back in 1895). So this is something I will never forget. It was a tremendous experience for me.

Dr Tom Potsik

USA

Miracles come in moments. Be ready and willing.

Dr Wayne W. Dyer

We Raced Through the Streets Of Lima

Working as a chiropractor in Lima, the capital city of Peru offers unique opportunities to take care of many types of people. When most people think of South American countries, they automatically think of the poor. What most people do not understand is that there exists an extremely wealthy section of society.

I had an extremely busy office, seeing clients six days a week. I often worked all day and late into the evening. It was not uncommon for me to see one thousand people during the week. I felt so blessed to be placed into an area where I could help so many people with chiropractic care.

It was usual for our office to be full beyond capacity with people in the waiting rooms and out in front of the building. My secretaries normally never bothered me with calls. One afternoon my secretary told me that there was a call I had to take. She informed me that a Colonel at the Peruvian Pentagon who wanted to talk to me. I told her I would call him back and please schedule a time for him to come in and meet me. She was a little flustered as she explained "You don't understand doctor, for security reasons this Colonel cannot come to see you. You must go to the pentagon to see him." She added that "you must not refuse an invitation from the Colonel!"

I had no idea of how powerful military leaders were in Peru at this point in time.

You can imagine my surprise when thirty five minutes later twelve armed men showed up in front of my office to pick me up. First were the two police motorcycles with sirens blaring, then a lead car with four heavily armed men, followed by my car, a Mercedes sedan with driver and guard, then a car to follow us, again loaded with four armed men.

I was whisked away by this armed escort. I was relieved they seemed happy to see me. When we arrived at the Pentagon we passed through a series of check points. At each stop the driver told the guard I was "the chiropractor" who seemed like the magic word because we were saluted and told to go on. We passed through a total of seven security checkpoints and I began to realize that this was no ordinary "Colonel."

We finally arrived at a huge door and an armed doorman came to the side of the car and opened the door for me. He escorted me to a huge, richly decorated mahogany walled office. From a side room a door slid open and out came a man in his late fifties dressed in a bright red jumpsuit and sparkling white tennis sneakers.

"So you're the doctor that everyone is talking about? You look kind of young to be a doctor!!!"

I thanked him for the compliment and received a handshake from a fist of steel.

Miracles of Health & Healing

He showed me to a back room that was like a large private hospital. It was filled with physiotherapeutic machines. "See all this Doctor?" he said with a wave of his hands pointing to the array of machines. "I have spent over one hundred thousand dollars and I still can't get well." His head suddenly whipped around and he focused fully on me as if seeing me for the first time.

"What do you think you can do for me?"

By shear auto response I blurted out "I can check your spine for misaligned bones that may be putting pressure on your nerves and limiting your innate capacity to heal and function optimally."

I don't think he had any idea of what I had just said, but his response said it all.

"I will do anything at this point. I have been suffering from low back pain for years and it continues to get worse. I am losing the feeling in my legs and other areas. The doctors here say that I need surgery but I don't trust those butchers. What do we need to do to start?"

Again I blurted out by auto response, "I will need you to come to my office so I can get some specific chiropractic X-rays."

His face lit up with a smile. "Great, let's go!" The entire entourage of security accompanied us as we raced through the streets of Lima with sirens blaring. As we got close to my office I noticed the roads around my office had been blocked off. I turned to the Colonel and said… Why do you have so much security Colonel?"

"Colonel!" He said, "I am not a Coronel, I am the Chairman of the Joint Chiefs of Staff for the entire military. My counterpart in your country is General Colin Powell!"

Thankfully he laughed and then we both laughed and entered the office together. The General had been a decorated paratrooper for many years and all those jumps had wreaked havoc with his lower spine. The discs spaces were practically gone and the bones were beginning to fuse.

I sat him down for a lay lecture with his four armed guards. I explained chiropractic to him and then gave him his first chiropractic adjustment. I explained that the adjustment would restore the proper alignment of his misaligned bones, removing the pressure from the nerves. I explained that slowly but surely his innate capacity to heal would be restored and he would have the best chance to be well. He was faithful in his visits, and began to come in a single car with only three bodyguards. After a few months his physical capacities began to improve. One day he came in and warmly shook my hand and told me he had just had the pleasure of telling his staff of surprised physicians that chiropractic care had saved him from the operating table!

I will never forget his statement about the one hundred thousand dollars of useless machines. He and I both learned from this experience that nothing is more powerful than the innate healing capacity of the body.

Chiropractic restores the miracle of life!

Dr Liam P Schubel

Peru

> *You will find as you look back upon your life that the moments when you have really lived are the moments when you have done things in the spirit of love.*
>
> *Henry Drummond*

Dr John Hinwood

The Miracle Provider

Recently I had the honour of speaking at the funeral of a beautiful woman Doreen Stevenson. Doreen was eighty nine years young when she passed on from this world and few were present on her funeral day due to estranged family happenings.

It was a joy to be able to share with those present of the miracles Doreen had created for my family and the members of our practice team.

On a hot and humid summer's day in sub-tropical Brisbane, Australia in February of 1981, Doreen Stevenson presented to our chiropractic practice with long standing lower back pain that had affected her for most of her adult life. She had had extensive spinal surgery, many years before, with no positive result and had been hospitalised for lengthy periods in the past and continually experienced wretched pain during her waking hours.

In 1981 we were new to Brisbane and Doreen had heard about successes people had experienced at our practice and she thought she would 'give us a go'. We had studied in Canada and there were only a couple of other chiropractors in our part of Australia at that time with Canadian training. Doreen felt Canadian training was very special.

On her initial visit Doreen said her pain had been

Miracles of Health & Healing

made worse that morning, because she had baked lots of family size apple pies and she had been standing at the kitchen bench for hours leaning forward.

In my typical jovial manner I asked her, "well, where is my apple pie?"

Her answer was something like, "I'm sorry, I didn't think to bring you one".

This off the cuff fun request started a gifting program from Doreen Stevenson that commenced on her visit the following day and only ended when we sold our practice fourteen years later.

This woman's gratitude for the care she received at our practice was truly amazing. She was the most prolific giver I have ever met. She was continually creating small miracle gifts for our team members.

On her second visit, Doreen made sure that she called a station wagon taxi as she delivered a gift of sixteen large family apple pies all made from scratch that morning. She made her own pastry, cooked the apples, ground the spices and added 'loads of love' to each pie. Her pies were scrumptious!! And they didn't stop coming for fourteen years!!!

Doreen loved cooking and was in the class of gifted cooks. She also made butterfly fresh cream cup cakes loaded with icing sugar, special apricot and rosella jam, pickles and lemon butter - all in copious quantities. She would also bring me cases of fresh figs in season grown by an elderly Italian gentleman.

Not only could Doreen cook, she loved her craft work and made our family members beautiful crochet rugs of all shapes, sizes and colours.

These rugs still adorn couches and beds in our home during the winter months almost thirty years after they were made. Doreen always used high quality wool. She had a friend who made the most amazing clowns and in 1985 when we adopted our three children from Chile, Doreen made sure they all had their own very special clown. I was President of the Australian Spinal Research Foundation for eight years and during that time, each year Doreen would donate several clowns for our annual ASRF Monster Raffle.

Doreen Stevenson taught me the power of gratitude and unconditional giving. She was a lady on the aged pension when she first came to our practice in 1981 and due to her severe spinal condition; she needed supportive care three visits per week. During all those years she always paid for her visits. She was offended when I suggested that I waive her visit fees because of her outstanding gifting. Her gifts she considered were a special thank you for all the love and caring our entire team showered her with on every visit.

Doreen Stevenson spent her life giving to others and she was truly a 'miracle provider'.

Dr John Hinwood, Australia

> *To understand the heart and mind of a person, look not at what he has already achieved, but what he aspires to.*
> — *Khalil Gibran*

Dr John Hinwood

6

MIRACLES OF HOPE

Do not be too timid and squeamish about your actions. All life is an experiment. The more experiments you make the better. What if they are a little coarse and you may get your coat soiled or torn?

What if you do fail, and get fairly rolled in the dirt once or twice.

Up again, you shall never be so afraid of a tumble.

Ralph Waldo Emerson

My Miracle Dream

Good morning John, my name is Matteo Capellino, I am an Italian man, and I live in Phuket, Thailand with my family. You will never believe what I am about to tell you.

About a month ago, I had a dream one night. I was actually quite impressed by it because it was really intense, so I told my wife about my very vivid dream the next morning.

In this dream, I was in a room with my wife and my daughter and we were talking and playing together. Some other people were also in the room looking at us in a reproaching way, as we were disturbing them. After a while, these people went out of the room, and the last man to leave spoke some words in Italian to us in a kindly way, as he wanted us to know that he'd been able to understand what we were talking about earlier, as we were speaking in Italian.

After that, I went out of the room as well, and found the man on the balcony. This balcony was quite high, and had a wonderful view of a big surrounding area. The man looked at me and I looked at him. He was tall, large-bodied and with big hands, wearing a blue jacket and a white shirt. We just shook hands very slowly, and looked peacefully into each other's eyes. What really impressed me was the deepness of his eyes. After a short time, my wife came out as well, and he just put his hand on her head, and because she was feeling a strong sense of protection, she closed her eyes and put her head on his chest in a genuine way, as if this man was her father.

The dream finished like this. Then, about two weeks ago, I was having a coffee in a coffee shop near our home and I bought the local newspaper, *The Phuket Gazette*. I was relaxing and reading it with my coffee, turning the pages one at a time when suddenly I felt as though I was dreaming with my eyes wide open, and in that moment I probably looked like a man who had seen a ghost. There in front of me on the page of the newspaper was the man I'd dreamed about two weeks earlier. His deep eyes were looking at me in the same way as they had in my dream.

Guess who the man in that picture in the newspaper was? It was Dr John Hinwood! I read the article about you coming to Phuket as the keynote speaker for the *Phuket Fitness and Wellness Festival*, and about your amazing *Expect A Miracle* cards.

Even more impressive is the fact that at this moment, it is probably the most difficult period in my life economically, and it is really a miracle that I am expecting to receive a miracle at this time to turn things around. Every time I look at the picture of you in the newspaper or on your website, it is really amazing to me. I really hope to see you during your visit to Phuket, and please let me know on Facebook what you think about this amazing fact.

With much affection.

Matteo Capellino

Thailand

Post Script

I met Matteo on May 7, 2012 in Phuket when he attended my first evening seminar presentation on Creating Miracles in Your Life. He also attended my other two Phuket events.

> *Without leaps of imagination, or dreaming, we lose the excitement of possibility. Dreaming, after all, is a form of planning.*
>
> *Gloria Steinem*

A Powerful Tool in Essence

Magicians use them to bedazzle us, fortune tellers can read our future through them, and children play with them for fun. They are used to identify us, to celebrate an occasion, to give us hope, to make us feel loved, and sometimes they are used to keep use on track with a cue. Regardless, one could say the humble card is certainly understated and unappreciated. What a powerful yet simple invention! Mr Miracle Man, Dr John Hinwood, certainly showed me how powerful the card can be.

As a professional realtor, the auction room is the best place to get business done. It is often full of intense emotion, and anything can happen.

Three essential ingredients are required to achieve a sale – a seller, a buyer, and the will by both parties to move forward and agree on an unconditional deal. Recently during an extended auction negotiation, I was in discussion with three potential buyers. The highest purchaser decided to pull out after three hours of negotiating, by which time the other two parties had lost hope of securing the property and left the building to drive home.

John saw I was running uphill and in need of a little inspiration. He gave me one of his *Expect A Miracle* cards and said to me, "Mason, this little card will make all the difference." It certainly put a smile on my face, and gave me the essential motivational lift I needed. Instead of pondering the loss of the buyers, it provided me with the inspiration to clear my mind, and get one of the potential buyers across the line by pondering the possibilities and thinking outside the box. I rang the family of conditional buyers who had left the building and were driving home. Miraculously, they came back, and we hammered out an unconditional deal that worked for everyone.

A simple card in appearance and a powerful tool in essence, is what this card represents. Miracles are all around us. We just need to recognize them and appreciate them when they happen.

Mason Garten

Australia

> *Great works are performed not by strength but by perseverance.*
>
> — *Samuel Johnson*

New Hope in His Life

I heard John speak at the Reconnection Seminar in Hamburg, Germany and he gave me an Expect A Miracle card. That evening, my taxi driver seemed very depressed and said that he had no hope in his life. He said that he had a sad experience last month. I took out the Expect A Miracle card and gave it to him. He said, "I don't believe in miracles anymore". My reply, "they are real". He said, "I should respect you".

The ice breaker of me giving him the card enabled him to start speaking about his view on miracles and spirituality. When we arrived at my home and I paid him double the cab fare. He said "no, no". My reply, "this is a miracle maybe". And he said "maybe there are other miracles". We spoke for about half an hour together and we were laughing and talking. We exchanged addresses and he said next time you come back to Hamburg I will show you the town and will tell you an exercise I know to tranquilize your mind. He was fun company and very happy to talk to and laugh with.

It was a complete transformation, because to start with he was like there was no chance in life for him. After me giving him an Expect A Miracle card, and then a miracle fare, he stated talking, sharing laughing, having fun and enjoying himself. He was now a changed man and full of hope.

I was happy about the gift I gave him.

Erika

Germany

> *Miracles happen to those who believe in them.*
>
> *Bernard Berenson*

Free Hugs

We were travelling back to the airport from our hotel after a recent Chiropractic seminar. Our driver was a gruff, abrupt man who was obviously in a hurry! Our team was with us and, with spirits on a high, we all sang and laughed our way to our destination.

The taxi driver who could speak only a little English stopped the car a hundred metres away from our designated drop-off. We were all wondering what was happening, he suddenly said that in three years of driving a taxi, he had never heard so much laughter and fun in his cab. "You are amazing!" he said. He then contrasted our team with those who were going on holiday but looked so glum and downtrodden with life that even a break 'away from it all' would appear to be a futile experience.

As we got out of the taxi, our team offered the driver 'free hugs'! He duly accepted and went on his way with a chuckle after receiving his miracle!

Dr Ross McDonald
Scotland

> *Often people attempt to live their lives backwards: they try to have more things, or more money, in order to do more of what they want so they will be happier. The way it actually works is the reverse. You must first be who you really are, then do what you love to do, in order to have what you want.*
>
> Margaret Young

Every Day Is A Miracle

I moved to Australia a few years ago from Miami, Florida having spent most of my life living in the north east of the United States. My miracle story is about how I came to spend those years living in Australia.

Until I was twenty five years of age, I felt like someone's miracle story would have to be about some dramatic event that happened in their life, that they were saved or they survived a tragedy but it wasn't until that point that I realised that every day is a miracle.

I went through a period in my life where I was married, then went through a separation and what I felt like should have been the worst time of my life, where I should have been feeling depressed, I should have been feeling a victim. I met some new people who opened my eyes to what is possible and so I grabbed that opportunity of a relationship ending and I started to create a new relationship with myself.

I took some time to travel as I had never travelled before. I spent some time in Europe then a few months in Australia and then went back to the United States. On the plane coming back from Europe I realised that I could do anything in the world that I wanted to do and now was a great opportunity to really achieve it. So I got off that plane and quit my job and started interviewing everyone I knew as to what was their miracle story and what gave them hope and satisfaction every day and through that I realised that I wanted to be a chiropractor and I feel that that choice is my miracle as it changed my life.

I moved to Australia after having spent four years living in California going to Chiropractic College. I met some amazing people through my travels, including my current partner while in Switzerland, and to welcome her and her awesome son into my life has been like living a dream.

That experience, for me, was very soul searching. Ending a relationship that was difficult wasn't a positive experience and here I am having the time of my life with people that I really love, so I expect and keep on expecting future miracles to come into my life.

Dr Derek Gallant

USA

Interesting, I think there is one thing that has killed more dreams, have kept more people from accomplishing more goals than death itself, and that's a person's concern about what others think.

Charles Henderson

7

MIRACLES OF LESSONS IN LIFE

Life if part positive and part negative.

Suppose you went to hear a symphony orchestra and all they played were the little, happy, high notes?

Would you leave soon?

Let me hear the rumble of the base, the crash of the symbols, and the minor keys.

Jim Rohn

I Was At Rock Bottom

I, like many of you, was raised in what is known today as a dysfunctional family, with an authoritarian father and a mother who was a guilty giver, hardly the nurturing and loving support system a child would have selected had they had the chance to choose parents that would guide them in more positive ways.

Anyway, despite the way I was raised, I graduated from college, became a chiropractor, got married, and had two children. Then, I found that I was 29 years of age and nothing was working in my life. My marriage wasn't working, I was doing poorly financially, my practice was lousy, and I didn't have a very good self image.

Then I went to a seminar, having never been to one before. It was something about positive thinking and motivation, and I literally had to be dragged there, but a miracle happened to me at that seminar. I walked in as a person really, really at the bottom of the barrel, and I walked out with a concept, an idea, a pathway, that if other people could be successful, healthy and happy, then so could I. I learned that, from that day on, if I started to write down goals and read them repeatedly, read books, listen to tapes, and meet with people who could pick me up and nurture me and encourage me to move on, I too could be successful. I trained my mind and visited people over the next few years, and eventually became a completely different person.

I went on to build several successful businesses, and now I spend my life helping other people to succeed, be happier, and develop a good self image.

You really can Expect A Miracle, because I didn't expect one, but I got one anyway.

Isn't it wonderful that nature takes care of us in this way? I encourage you to Expect A Miracle, to think big, to write down some goals, do some affirmations, let go gracefully from stale relationships, surround yourself with nurturing and uplifting people, and know there is a plan for you that can lead you to health, happiness, wealth, success and fulfillment in life.

Dr Larry Markson

USA

> *You've got to walk right into what you want and not look at what you don't want. Stay focused on the goal.*
>
> *Calvin LeHew*

The Speeding Ticket Miracle

Last October, while driving into Los Angeles I was stopped for speeding in Indio. I had my miracle card right on the dash, so when the officer took my documents I went into "I could use a miracle now!" The officer came back and gave me a ticket without any consideration of dropping the speed a bit, but let me off on the fact that I had no documents for proof of insurance or registration. Oops. Not really a notable miracle, but off I went.

Before I go on, I would like to mention that when I share the miracle card, I say the universe is abundant with them, so allow them to flow please.

After about thirty minutes, I rounded a curve on I-10 past San Bernardino and suddenly there was nothing but brake lights in front of me in all lanes. I had stopped speeding once I got that ticket earlier, by the way, so I was travelling at the speed limit or safe speed for the traffic conditions now.
Even before my foot hit the brakes, I knew that I was not going to be able to stop in time. I was driving a pickup truck with a large trailer behind me carrying massage tables for *The Reconnection's* upcoming seminars. My next thought after realizing I could not stop was, Is someone going to die? As these thoughts were running through my head, and I was in a state of

Miracles of Lessons in Life

what seemed like stillness, my head turned to the left and I saw nothing but dark, empty space, and my truck literally moved over with grace and ease.

Whenever there is a traffic jam, one would generally look to see what the cause of the stopped traffic was when they eventually reached it. I do not even remember noticing anything to do with the stopped traffic. I just remember the realization that I was moving in grace and ease, and continuing my drive.

When I paid that traffic ticket for $550, I was actually grateful for the traffic cop, who had at least brought me back to a responsible speed.

If I had not been stopped for speeding, and taken a breather to contemplate a miracle, perhaps there would not have been one. Thank you officer for giving me the speeding ticket. You were a life-saver that day.

Renee Coltson

USA

There is no shortcut to life. To the end of our days, life is a lesson imperfectly learned.

Harrison E. Salisbury

Dr John Hinwood

Every Day Something Lucky, Fortunate, Miraculous Happens

Thanks you John, my Expect A Miracle (EAM) cards arrived yesterday. So many! So many more to hand out! As I mentioned, I have them planted all over the place, with one in my purse. Every day something lucky, fortunate, miraculous happens. Like yesterday, when I was wearing my favourite sterling silver ring that I bought from a French silversmith at a gallery in Margaret River last year. I was in a shop when I heard a ping on the floor. I picked up what I thought looked like a silver button, but alas, it was part of my ring. Where was the rest of it? The shop assistant was lovely, and moved display cases and crawled around the floor for ages. Oh well, I'm thinking ... it's only stuff! I reached into my shopping bag to put something else in and ... EAM! There was the other piece of the ring.

The jeweller said it could easily be fixed; in fact, he would fix it so that it would never happen again. So there you go. Of course, that was what I would call a "minor" miracle. Many more seriously important good things have happened as well.

Paula Byrnes

Australia

> Be enthusiastic about your decision. It is your decision!
>
> Reach, seek, risk! Don't ever stop.
>
> Follow your thoughts and don't listen to others.
>
> It is your life and you'll get it ... You Can Do It.
>
> Sir Leny Rodrigues Garcia

Who Was That Guy?

While attending a seminar in Sydney, Australia recently, an interesting coincidence happened; or possibly there is an organisation to our universe.

I and my business partner Josie were up early on the Sunday morning. Our staff was going to join us for breakfast, so we decided to go for a walk around Darling Harbour next to the Sydney Convention Centre to find a suitable restaurant for us to eat at, from the myriad of restaurants available.

As it was 7 am, there were very few people around. While walking along the wharf we saw Drs John & Judy Hinwood walking towards us. I had seen John a few times at the seminar we were both attending, but he was always with someone or other of the more than eight hundred in attendance, and we hadn't had an opportunity to catch up. As we got within about twenty metres of each other, we put our arms out to give each other an 'air hug' greeting and carried on walking towards each other.

As we came together, John hugged me and kissed me on either cheek, his usual loving greeting. As we released each other, I noticed there was another guy standing within a couple of metres of us and off to my right side. He was just looking at us. I assumed he knew John, and was waiting for us to finish our greeting so he could converse with him.

As we broke our embrace, he looked at John and said, "I would like one of those please, without the kiss." When invited in for a hug, John will never say no, but the recipient doesn't dictate the terms, so the guy gets the full treatment – a hugely embracing hug and a kiss on each cheek.

At this point in time, John assumed the guy was with me, and I was being rude in not introducing him. Once he had received his hug and the kisses that went with it, he walked into the adjacent restaurant and sat down.

John, Judy, Josie and I had a brief conversation and we parted ways. Josie and I were laughing at how this random person had seen two men hugging and kissing as a greeting and had felt such a connection that he was strong enough to ask for a hug. Is the rest of the world out there so lacking in human contact those they walk up to hugging strangers and ask to be included?

We continued walking along the harbour front, but not finding a suitable breakfast menu, turned around to go back the way we had come. As we were walking back past the restaurant where this had happened, we were engaged in our own conversation. Next, we heard, "Excuse me?" We looked into the restaurant, and it was the same guy sitting having a coffee, gesturing us over.

We walked over to him. "Who was that guy?" he asked. I had assumed that he was a chiropractor from the seminar we were attending at the Sydney Convention Centre who had recognized John and wanted the signature "Hinwood Hug." It then dawned on me that he was just a person off the street, and the significance of his act increased in my mind considerably.

"Oh, he's a chiropractor," I said.

"Really?" he replied. "I am a chiropractor too! I retired fifteen years ago and bought this restaurant. This is mine," he proudly proclaimed, waving his arms around the restaurant.

"So you are not at the seminar at the Convention Centre?" I asked.

"I don't know of any seminar, I am a restaurateur," he said, "What seminar?"

"The biggest chiropractic seminar in the country is on here in Sydney at the moment, and we are delegates. Do you know Dr John Hinwood?" I asked, thinking that every chiropractor in Australia and New Zealand does know him ... particularly the ones who ask for hugs.

"Oh no," he said, "I'm long retired. I should have dropped off fliers for my restaurant."

What was the chance? Some random individual sees two men hugging, asks if he can be part of it – then it turns out he is a retired chiropractor himself and just happened to be there at that

Miracles of Lessons in Life

moment in time with a need for a man hug and happy to ask for it.

The miracle of a hug is just so healing, and it brings so much joy into the lives of the receiver and the giver

Dr Brett Ireland

Australia

> *The world is a great miracle. It reflects back to you what you see. If you love, if you are friendly, if you are helpful, the world will prove loving and friendly and helpful to you.*
>
> *The world is what you are.*
>
> *Thomas Dreier*

Dr John Hinwood

He Assumed a State Of Being

I'm writing this note from a video recording I made for Dr Hinwood, sharing a life-changing miracle that occurred in my life. I'm doing this sitting beside the beach in beautiful Phuket, Thailand. It's a tropical paradise. I live here with my youngest son who is completing high school. My eldest son completed high school last year and he has returned to Australia to build his own life. I have a blossoming business and I've been in a loving relationship for the last four years. Let me tell you though, that life has not always been this good.

In the early '90's I was very excited to be offered a promotion and went with the hotel group I was working for to Vanuatu, another tropical paradise. In the years I spent in Vanuatu I went on to manage hotel properties and was eventually a partner in a beautiful beachfront resort. There I was in my early 30's, I felt like I'd made it. We had a kilometre of beachfront, eighty acres of land on the beach, life was great. We had two yachts as it was a boost for my ego; I purchased a new vehicle each year, and travelled regularly.

But... there was something that wasn't right. I was unhappy in my marriage, and I didn't really feel like I had a sense of purpose. Let me tell you that from the peak of my "success", it didn't take too long for things to unravel. By the end of the

'90's I was living in Brisbane, in my mother in law's basement. Shortly thereafter I was bankrupt. Two years later I was divorced. My children lived with their mother, and I was lost.

I was working as a casual waiter, back where I began. I'd climbed the corporate ladder in hospitality, and then descended far more swiftly than I had climbed it. From being a general manager of international hotel properties, then owning a resort property, and now back to being a waiter. I'd lost my confidence and my certainty, but I still retained my ignorance and arrogance.

The miracle began when I stopped trying. I stopped trying to be cool. I stopped trying to be rich. I stopped trying to be first. I stopped trying to be right. I stopped trying to be perfect. I stopped trying to be something that I wasn't.

And I began to practice being.

Being kind, being willing to understand, being willing to serve, being open, being generous, and being humble. As a consequence wonderful things started coming to me, and continue to come to me.

When I reflect and look back, and think about my bankruptcy and my divorce, the years without my children, these were in fact great blessings. In fact my harsh creditors, my former wife, my isolation, these were all great teachers to me and I'm very, very thankful for those experiences. Without these, I would have continued my shallow and miserable existence, without even knowing what it was.

I couldn't have said this a few years ago, because I certainly wasn't grateful or appreciative at that time. But as I practiced being more humble, my mind opened to the point where I could begin to investigate and observe what was happening in my life. I discovered that simplicity, honesty and truthfulness were all that I really needed. Yes, I still want to have a Ferrari, but it's not a burning desire, and it does not drive me. There are miracles in my life every day, one of the most significant so far that I have experienced is learning to stop trying and just be.

My greatest wish for you as you read this is that you too will be able to see all the amazing miracles that happen in your life every day. And appreciate and understand them as miracles.

Michael Massey

Thailand

Editors Footnote:

Michael owns and operates perhaps the one of most well regarded wellness resorts in the world. I have facilitated courses there; I have personally experienced one of Atmanjai's seven day detox programs. It's a special place.

Miracles of Lessons in Life

I met Michael when he was bankrupt in his 'down and out' days in Brisbane and got to know him personally and know of his great passion for motorsport. In October 2012 Michael did not get his dream Ferrari, but he was invited to be a guest in the pits of the Ferrari Team at the Indian Formula 1 Grand Prix in appreciation of his services to one of their key executives. He and his sons were in India at that time to attend the Grand Prix as the personal guests of the Mercedes Benz distributors for India, again in appreciation of his services to one of their key executives.

From being bankrupt and living in his mother in laws basement to hobnobbing with the elite of world motorsport is a miracle in itself. All made possible in Michael's words, "by simply being... not trying."

> *Cease trying to work everything out with your minds, it will get you nowhere. Live by intuition and inspiration and let your whole life be a revelation.*
>
> *Eileen Caddy*

Dr John Hinwood

8

MIRACLES OF SPORT

All your life you are told the things you cannot do. All your life they will say you are not good enough or strong enough or talented enough; they will say you are the wrong height or the wrong weight or the wrong type to play this or be this or achieve this.

THEY WILL TELL YOU NO, a thousand times no, until all the no's become meaningless. All your life they will tell you no, quite firmly and very quickly.

AND YOU WILL TELL THEM ... YES!

Nike Ad

Dr John Hinwood

My First Rugby International

Playing rugby union football in my childhood, at college and then in my adult years until I was thirty-four years old was always sheer joy for me.

When I met my wife Judy, she also loved watching rugby, and we have been fortunate in our travels to have seen some awesome rugby internationals played at famous rugby grounds around the world.

As a family, we all love rugby, and on adopting our three older children, Shavela, Nat and Rod from Chile in 1985, we immediately introduced them to share one of our passions in life. Nat and Rod both played at school and into their adult life until travel, business and their own family life took centre stage. Now, we still get together and either go to the big games or watch them on TV.

In late April of 1970, after months of travelling overland from Australia through Asia, Eastern Europe and Western Europe, we arrived in Denmark to work and spend some time with my wife's sister Carlie and her Danish husband Andrew.

Being a physical education teacher, active sportsman and sports coach in those days meant that I was ready to get back into playing some sport when I arrived in Denmark. Part of my physical education teacher training was gaining four referees tickets in different sports. Rugby was

Miracles of Sport

one sport I held a ticket in and, totally unbeknown to me on arriving in Denmark, this would prove to be a miracle stepping stone for me.

The day we arrived in Copenhagen, I looked in the Yellow Pages and found five clubs in the city and three clubs in other parts of Denmark. *Rugby Club Speed* was the closest to where we were living, so I called the club secretary and was invited to training the next night.

How much fun I had on that first night at training with all the coaching in Danish via my translator. The club members were all Danes and so welcoming that I felt immediately at home. The lads were all good drinkers too, and enjoyed drinking some 'ool', beer in Danish, and singing all the great rugby songs in the Queen's English after our heavy training session. I was told at training that night that they could see I was a very experienced player, and I was invited to join the first's team.

There were no club fixtures the next Saturday, as it was the anniversary of twenty years of Danish Rugby, and the national team was playing an International match against a team representing the other three Scandinavian countries to celebrate the anniversary.

As there were only eight clubs in Denmark, and the sport had a negligible following, all the players and their families from around the country would come together on the day to support their national team. Rugby had recently

Dr John Hinwood

been introduced into the Danish high school system, so they were also expecting a good turnout of schoolboys for the match.

At 11am on the day of the game, I received a phone call from Jurgen, our club secretary, who was also the secretary of the Danish Rugby Union. He was quite concerned that the neutral referee they had flown in from England the previous night had woken with a major gastric and vomiting attack and was in no way able to take the field to referee the Test match. In a very hesitant manner, Jurgen asked me would I consider acting as the match referee in three hours' time.
WOW ... only four days in Denmark, and I'm elevated from refereeing schoolboy rugby in Australia to a Rugby International in Europe! A rugby miracle!

The Danish Rugby Referees Association kitted me out and I had my day. And what a day it was.

After the match, I was one of the special guests at the pucker Anniversary Celebration Dinner at a beautiful five-star Copenhagen hotel. Together with both captains, I was presented with a special commemorative plate that had been struck by the famous Danish porcelain makers Bing & Grondahl to celebrate the occasion. The plate sits on a shelf in my study forty-one years later.

Another miracle happened that night. At the dinner, I was seated next to the Chief Inspector of Schools for Physical Education in Copenhagen. When he found out I was a physical education teacher in Australia and I was a Senior Examiner of The Royal Life Saving Society, he immediately offered me the position of Chief Swimming Instructor for Copenhagen Schools. Previously, the Danish Ministry for Education had told me my teaching qualifications were not of a high enough standard to teach in Denmark.

The miracles didn't stop there that evening. The Danish Rugby Union was seeking a new national coach that season, with a preference for a player-coach. Their rules allowed for a non-Danish national to fill this role. My one training session with my new club and the great job I did refereeing the International that day was enough for the President of the Danish Rugby Union to offer me the appointment. I immediately accepted.

One man's brief health challenge that day opened the door for me to receive three miracles in a twenty-four-hour period. I was elated!

Dr John Hinwood

Australia

> *You have to participate relentlessly in the manifestation of your blessings.*
>
> — Elizabeth Gilbert

I Didn't Have Any Direction in My Life

Back in early 2009, I met Dr John Hinwood, a family friend of my father. Over dinner, he explained to me the significance of a lone card he kept in his wallet. It was an Expect A Miracle card.

He explained that Expect A Miracle was a project he had been working on for years which spread hope and good fortune.

I had discussed with him how I didn't have any direction in my life, and things seemed to be at a standstill. He handed me an Expect A Miracle card, and from that day on there was momentum in my life. By the end of the year, I had been appointed Sports Captain in my House at school and led my House to their first-ever second place against twelve other Houses in their twenty-five-year history.

The following year I was appointed Gymnastics Captain, and against all odds finished second in Australia, placing me on the Australian Gymnastics Team, and then later out school team won the Greater Public Schools gymnastics tournament, making it our first-ever hat-trick in our school's one-hundred-year history.

All it took was for me to look at and focus on that one card with those magical words, Expect A Miracle, before every major event in my life. To this day, that card remains in my wallet and continues to bless me in life.

I'm thankful that Dr John Hinwood is making the extra effort just to make people's lives more enjoyable, and glad to know that regardless of who you are, there is someone out there who cares about you enough to change your life, like he changed mine.

Thank you, Dr Hinwood, for your help so far, and I can't wait to get stuck into my studies to one day become the best chiropractor on the Gold Coast.

Brandon Clift

Australia

> *Focus more on your desire than on your doubt, and the dream will take care of itself. You may be surprised how easily this happens. Your doubts are not as powerful as your desires, unless you make them so.*
>
> *Marcia Wieder*

9

MIRACLES OF WORK

The work of the individual still remains the spark that moves mankind forward.

Igor Sikorsky

Dr John Hinwood

How Did You Find Me?

In the late 1970s, I started chiropractic practice in Australia in a small rural community north of Sydney. I came across a wonderful question to ask all my new patients who had not come to see me by personal referral from a family member, friend or other health professional.

In those days, most practices were made up of 70 percent new patients who were referred and 30 percent who found their way to the practice by seeing your sign or Yellow Page listing in the phone directory. Most of this group came from the phone book listing.

At the annual National Chiropractic Conference that year, I met a wonderful chiropractor from Perth, Western Australia by the name of Dr Michael McKibbin. We happened to sit beside each other at lunch, and he shared with me his 'ice breaker' that he used when greeting patients for the first time who were not specifically referred to him.

His opening question was, "Did you find me in the phone book under C for Chiropractic or M for Miracle?"

He said it always brought a laugh, or at least a chuckle, from the new patient, and he was off to a great start with this new person.

I thought this was excellent, and immediately

adopted the idea into my daily practice routine.

Almost every person I've asked this of has said, "C for Chiropractor, but M for Miracle would be so much better." Then I would point to the Expect A Miracle sign on the wall in my consulting room and they would laugh and say, "Oh, yeh."

In 1987, I started handing out an Expect A Miracle card to every new patient to give them an attitude boost, so we could move forward together in a positive way on their healing journey.

Dr John Hinwood

Australia

> *The true self is always in motion like music, a river of life, changing, moving, failing, suffering, learning and shining.*
>
> *Brenda Ueland*

Put Out the Energy

Have you ever been thinking about one of your clients and the next thing you know they... appear in your appointment book, or; you hear the chiropractic assistant taking a call from them, or; they stop in to say "Hi" or to make an appointment?

So many times, we hear stories like this. It even happens to the extent that a group of files can be taken out for recalls, and before the calls are even made, some of the people show up!

Recently, when I entered my favourite Indian restaurant, the waiter was overwhelmed to see me. He couldn't believe that during that very afternoon, he had been thinking of me.

I told him he had put the energy out there for me to show up. His reply was amazing. On a previous occasion, I had given him an Expect A Miracle card. He said, in a wonderful Indian accent, that he was expecting a 'mirackall'. We both laughed heartily! The point being that my Indian waiter, like you and your CAs had, as we called it, put out the energy.

By displaying a positive attitude and sending out good energy, it is possible to attract what we think about. If we do this with the right intention and with gratitude in advance for our clients, amazing results can happen.

Berni Ireland

Australia

> *Whatever we think about and thank about we bring about.*
>
> — Dr John F Demartini

Dr John Hinwood

Hit By a Bull

In early 1979 after opening our first chiropractic practice in the idyllic sea side town of Forster 300 kilometres north of Sydney; we quickly started getting many referrals from Gloucester, a small cattle town one hundred and ten kilometres to our west.

The constant flow of new clients from Gloucester prompted us to answer the call from many of the Gloucester folk that we open a branch practice there two days a week.

On Tuesday and Thursday while Judy worked at our home practice in Forster I would drive an hour each way to our Gloucester practice which was a newly renovated flat on top of Jack Burt's Shoe Store on the Buckets Way, Gloucester's main street. Jack was a Councillor on the local Shire Council and the Council of the day wanted the addition of chiropractic services for their community.

The Council gave me a special permit to practice in the spacious flat as there was nowhere in town that was available for rent.

My sign was on the main street at the shoe store entrance with a direction at the bottom that read... *Entrance at rear from car park*. There were twenty two steps that my patients needed to climb to reach me.

Miracles of Work

Having the practice entrance off the Council Car Park, which was a section of the main town park, was very handy during my two years in Gloucester. Two 'old boys' in their mid eighties would ride their horses to town and tie them up on the post and rail fence which surrounded the Car Park when they came for their adjustment visits.

My reason for practising in Gloucester on Tuesday and Thursday was that these were the days of the cattle sales and the three thousand population of the town really increased on sales days.

This beautiful little rural town is at the foot of Australia's Great Dividing Range, and is the gateway to a crossing through the rugged mountain range, over a very windy dirt road called the Thunderbolts Way. You rise from hilly country at the foot of the range and climb to the Northern Tablelands and then onto the western plains of New South Wales. Cattle trucks were a common site as you drove up and down this majestic road to go through the mountain pass.

One morning during my second month in Gloucester, my assistant Susan told me that she had just received a call from the local Ambulance Station that an ambulance was on its way to town with an extremely acute dairy farmer who did not want to be transported to the local hospital. He was insisting that he be brought to my office as he wanted chiropractic care for his problem. The dispatcher said they would be arriving in approximately twenty minutes.

The twenty minutes passed, then an hour went by and no ambulance arrived. As we were ready to finish for the lunch break, Susan came into my office to say she just saw the ambulance pull up in the car park downstairs.

Moments later two ambulance officers who were the stretcher bearers, appeared in our reception room with their patient. I went to welcome the dairy farmer with the extremely acute lower back problem. Alas, the patient on the stretcher was a third ambulance officer who was on his back with a large neck brace in place.

I asked the stretcher bearers, "Where is the farmer with the extremely bad lower back problem, we have been expecting?"

The answer, "oh, he's all fixed up now, but the severe impact of the collision has caused a major whiplash to our colleague who was driving the ambulance".

As I took the patients history he related to me a truly amazing story.

The ambulance driver was driving as fast as the road conditions would allow on the windy dirt road and was about ten kilometres out of town. Suddenly, a very large bull stormed out of a heavily timbered area beside the road and stopped directly in front of him, taking up the

Miracles of Work

entire road. The driver had nowhere to go.

The safest option the driver had, considering the rough terrain he was driving through, was to crash into the massive beast. On impact, which killed the poor bull, the force was so great that it sprung the back doors of the ambulance open .It projected the spinal board with the patient on it out into the air like a man being 'shot out of a cannon' at the circus.

The dairy farmer landed on the ground some sixty feet away with a resounding crash. On landing, the adrenalin, and who knows what other hormones, flowing through his system in a big way, kicked in immediately. The farmer sprang to his feet and raced to the ambulance to assist the driver who was trapped inside.

After getting the ambulance driver free of the wreck and making him as comfortable as possible by the roadside, he had an epiphany. The force of the impact and he being catapulted through the air and landing with a resounding thud on the ground sixty feet away had shifted something in his spine. The ambulance driver said his patient started dancing around shouting, "I'm cured, I'm cured!!"

The next thing to attend to was the severe whiplash suffered by the ambulance driver. The driver said that the patient with the writhing back pain was adamant that I would be able to 'cure'

Dr John Hinwood

his severe back problem and he was also sure I could cure the drivers whiplash.

The injured ambulance driver then said to me, "the logical place that they needed to take me to for care was Gloucester Chiropractic Centre to see you, exactly where we were heading in the first place."

Dr John Hinwood

Australia

> *Life's a pretty precious and wonderful thing. You can't sit down and let it lap around you... you have to plunge into it, you have to dive through it.*
>
> *Kyle Crichton*

Path to Life

In 2005 I was sitting in a conference in another part of the world, thinking about the situation for chiropractic in Spain. We only had at the time 150 chiropractors, 45 million people and no educational institutions for our profession. No law, what do we do?

It became extremely clear to me that my path was to open a Chiropractic College in Barcelona. However, every other time I ever had that thought previously; I had a lot of doubt around it. This time it seemed very clear to me that it was the way forward and my miracle was that within 24 hours of having made that decision and having that clear realization without accepting all of the excuses I made before, I was given a contact for a group of educational consultants who have offices in both London and Barcelona.

On contacting these consultants, that dream became a reality. As soon as I was crystal clear, the solution appeared and all my previous doubts that I had as my excuse for not going forward, just disappeared. My miracle wish became a reality.

Dr Adrian Wenban

Spain

> *It is often proved true that the dream of yesterday is the hope of today, and the reality of tomorrow.*
>
> — Dr Robert Goddard

Sixty Five Million Wheelchairs Needed Globally

I am proud to say I am blessed and have now found the courage and strength to give the world mobility in the form of wheelchairs.

On the 18th July 2009 I was sitting in the Mall in Brisbane, Australia and I noticed a little boy in an awkward, dated, old looking wheelchair. I thought why are wheelchairs still so horrible looking these days? Prams, strollers, bikes, even segways are so nice looking now, yet most wheelchairs are still so basic.

I thought I would design something so the wheelchairs would be more practical, fun and nice looking. I still have the drawing I did on that day of what I was going to have an engineer help build. I knew absolutely nothing about wheelchair design. After some research, I found a wheelchair just like I wanted to make, but get this, it cost $25,000. I thought that was shocking. Just over a year later I know so much more.

My focus has turned from having a good looking wheelchair to providing wheelchairs correctly made, and raising awareness of the needs of the riders. I am now on a mission to support those over sixty five million people globally who are in need of a wheelchair. These numbers are based on the World Health Organisation (W.H.O.) statistics. I launched a website to show the world my discoveries. As far as miracles go, I feel this is now my purpose. I am so passionate about giving the world mobility.

I went to Spain to do part of the Camino walk. I was soul searching and sharing the fact that we need so many wheelchairs. On the way home from Spain, sitting next to me were three lovely angels from Papua New Guinea (PNG), Joachim, Raphael and Andrew. I asked them what the wheelchair situation was like in PNG and they told me it is pretty shocking actually. I feel the universe is on a weekly and sometimes daily plan, giving me so many directions to help me raise awareness.

I told these three lovely angels that I was on a mission to change the shortage of wheelchairs. They were so excited that we planned to stay in touch and see how we could work together to help the people of PNG. I am proud to say that over the Christmas break 2010, I have now been invited by the locals of PNG to visit their country and I will be able to see for myself what we need to do.

Based on WHO statistics there are over 50,000 wheelchairs needed in PNG, Australia's closest neighbour. I now have a plan as to how we can help change this. I was having doubts about what I was doing earlier this year and another sign came from somewhere, another miracle you might say.

Miracles of Work

Most of my friends and colleagues at my work know I am on this mission. A wonderful angel from work, Sue called me on a Friday night as I was sitting thinking about what am I doing. Sue said to turn on the television quickly as there was a documentary about wheelchairs. It was about a group helping in Haiti called Whirlwind wheelchairs and they are part of the University of San Francisco. The following Monday I contacted this group and told them what I was doing. We kept in touch to see how we could work together. After I launched my website in May 2010, the University of San Francisco invited me to their campus in July where I test rode one of their *Rough Rider* wheelchairs. They are perfect for rough terrain such as PNG and our Australian outback.

The guys at the university, Ralph (the founder), Keoke, Marc, Matt, Bob, Peter and Aaron were so great to me. They shared what they are doing and I learnt so much. It is not just giving a wheelchair to someone; it is about providing the *correctly fitted* wheelchair for the person's condition. If you give the wrong size, shape etc. it could do damage, such as pressure sores, which can lead to blood poising and pain. We planned for us to all meet up in Indonesia late this year so we could see a sustainable, operating model for wheelchair provision really working .We will also visit a local wheelchair manufacturing company.

Dr John Hinwood

I met up with the men in Indonesia early in November to go to a wheelchair manufacturing plant where the chairs are made for a very reasonable price when bought in bulk. In Indonesia we also visited the United Cerebral Palsy - Wheels for Humanity (Indonesia) site at Yogyakarta. I am proud to have met Michael, a wonderful young man heading up their wheelchair project.

Michael has a sustainable, operating model for providing wheelchairs and nearly all their staff is local, some in wheelchairs. They were provided with a large area within a local university where they store the completed wheelchairs and then they have a local social worker who is in a wheelchair herself, the gorgeous angel, Sri, who goes out to visit children needing a wheelchair. They have modified Sri's motorcycle so it has a side car on it and she wheels up a little ramp and sits in her wheelchair. A photo will soon be up on my website.

It is so inspiring to see her ride around on this motorbike and in her wheelchair. It also gives other children and their families hope that they may be able do the same and get out and about and not just be stuck on the ground, or in a bed, and never go anywhere.

There are over 6 million children in Indonesia needing wheelchairs. Indonesia is a frequent holiday destination for Australians, but how many Aussies know that fact?

Miracles of Work

I am proud to be associated with Whirlwind Wheelchairs who have also put me in touch with Motivation Australia who provide correct training and delivery of wheelchairs globally. I have learnt so much from Kylie at Motivation and am in full support of helping raise awareness for what they are doing. I am now on a mission to raise funds to support their work.

I will be meeting up with Kylie's connections in PNG to see how we can all work together. I feel there are so many groups doing similar things that if we collaborate a little more we can be more efficient and effective as we are all wanting to give people a new life by providing the correct wheelchair. I am a connector and collaborator and my role is to bring us all together as a united team.

I was told by my PNG friends that in their village they still need toilets and things for their school. I am also proud to say that the wonderful Robina Rotary Club on the Gold Coast in Australia is now supporting the wheelchair project.

Today I was at my favourite pizza restaurant in Brisbane and met another person working in PNG. She offered to see if her group could possibly help us. I will be contacting them tomorrow. AMAZING... miracles just keep happening!!

Now I have a plan. Over the coming weeks I will be contacting many organisations to ask them to become involved with our work. I spoke with some senior people at my local Woolworths supermarket last week and they were not aware that so many people need wheelchairs globally. They said they would connect me to their community managers in each state. I so hope they do.

So many other amazing things have happened over the last year, miracles everywhere.

Helen Edwards

Australia

> *Your work is going to fill a large part of your life, and the only way to be truly satisfied is to do what you believe is great work. And the only way to do great work is to love what you do. If you haven't found it yet, keep looking. Don't settle. As with all matters of the heart, you'll know when you find it. And, like any great relationship, it just gets better and better as the years roll on. So keep looking until you find it. Don't settle.*
>
> *Steve Jobs*

Miracles of Work

They Were All Wearing Them

A few years ago my wife Judy and I were speaking at a conference on the Spanish island of Majorca. We arrived at Palma Airport late at night two days before the conference began. Then one of those travel hiccups you never want to experience, happened to us. Our bags were not on the baggage carousel.

Our journey had started some forty two hours earlier, initially with a train ride for an hour and a half from our home to Brisbane Airport on Australia's east coast. From there we flew to Singapore, changed planes and three hours later flew onto London. Then it took another few hours in transferring to a flight to Madrid, where after some delay, we once again transferred to a flight to our final destination. Palma is a beautiful city on the Mediterranean Sea.

After so long in the same clothes, we were very keen to shower, as it was the hot Spanish summer.

We waited and waited at the baggage carousel in the hope they would finally locate our lost baggage. To no avail, our bags were 'who knows where' at that point in time.

A helpful attendant escorted us to the lost luggage office. We were greeted by a friendly middle aged woman who spoke little English. We first had to identify our bags by pictures we were shown and then fill in the lost luggage claim form. As we had been on four different plane flights spanning some forty two hours and three continents, starting on the other side of the world, the claims clerk was not confident that our bags would be located in the near future!

My custom on meeting new people is to give them an *Expect A Miracle* card. Being close to midnight when we finally reached the friendly woman at the Lost Luggage Office, and being very tired, I initially forgot to give her a card. On realizing my lapse in personal protocol, I immediately reached into my pocket and gave the woman an *Expect A Miracle* card.

There was a look of instant wonderment that came to her face as she read those magical words. She smiled broadly and immediately disappeared to the back office from the front counter where she was tending us. She returned shortly after with the broadest of smiles and her Expect A Miracle card in a name card holder pinned to her chest. Not only that, she arrived with four other women who were the night shift crew and all were excited at the prospect that they all may also be able to receive their very own Expect A Miracle cards, as one of these women explained who had good English.

On receiving their Expect A Miracle cards they all disappeared out back for a shot time and appeared again with their cards in name tags holders they were wearing.

Miracles of Work

Our small army of carers went immediately to work and kept going to and fro from the counter to the back office bringing several changes of new articles of clothing including underwear, socks, pyjamas, shirts and toiletries plus numerous other goodies and a welcome cash handout. Our new support team assured us that they would find our luggage soon and create our miracle.

By the time we were kitted out at the airport and then made our way to our beautiful hotel, overlooking the extensive yacht marina in downtown Palma, it was approaching two am. The marina created an amazing display of fairy lights on the endless yachts moored there.

The hotel was a magnificent example of the old school of Five Star European hotels with grand appointments and furnishings to match. We were greeted by a well-dressed doorman and escorted to the registration desk.

It so happened that the Night Manager was at registration checking on something when we arrived and he and his two staff members gave us a special welcome, especially as we had no suite cases, and our only luggage was my carryon bag and we each had a plastic bag that our new found friends at the airport had given us.

They felt so sorry for us because we had travelled so far, over such a long period and our bags had been lost.

We thanked them for their genuine love and caring of us as we completed the registration cards. I whipped out four Expect A Miracle cards, three for the registration desk team and I briefly excused myself to take one to the doorman.

On my return to the front desk there was much excited chatter about the cards and the manager was busy attaching them to the jackets of his staff members and himself with paper clips. They all thought the gift was ever so special.

Their chatter changed from English to Spanish as they searched the room allocation roster. They wanted to find a deluxe luxury room for us overlooking the marina to give us a complementary upgrade.

The Manager personally escorted us to the most outstanding room and continually thanked me for the *Expect A Miracle* cards. Just before he left the room I asked him would he like cards for his entire staff. He was overwhelmed and immediately said, 'si Senior'. I asked him how many he needed and then produced them from my carryon bag. Gracias, gracias Senior!!

The next morning we went to late breakfast and all the staff in the hotel was wearing an Expect A Miracle card on their chest in a plastic badge holder.

That evening the Night Manager couldn't do

enough for us and told us that on our return to the hotel in five days time, he would have a special room for us to say thank you. We were leaving the next morning to travel to the other side of the island to speak at the seminar we had travelled to Majorca for.

On our return to this beautiful hotel we were welcomed like a King and Queen and given, at no extra charge, the Royal Suite as a gift of the management. We stayed there for the next seven days in the 'lap of the Gods'. Our balcony overlooking the magnificent harbor would have been big enough to entertain one hundred guests at a sit down dinner.

Yes, our bags did turn up the next morning before we left Palma to travel to the other side of the island. Miracles just do keep happening.

What joy these little cards brought so many souls in Palma that summer.

Dr John Hinwood

Australia

Expectancy is the atmosphere for miracles.

Edwin Louis Cole

Share Your Miracle Stories

Share your miracle stories with the rest of the world. If you have a miracle story of your own, or someone else's, that you feel would enhance the lives of others, please post it on www.expectamiracle.com.

The best stories each year will be in future volumes of **You Can Expect A Miracle**.

An added benefit of submitting your stories to the website is that you could **win prizes** if you are chosen as the winner of the **Readers' Choice Story of the Week, Month and Year**.

The most read story each week from all those that have previously not won a prize will be awarded the **Readers' Choice Story of the Week** and will be featured on www.expectamiracle.com.

Our Judging Panel will select the best story of the weekly winners of the previous month and the author will be awarded **Readers' Choice Story of the Month**.

Each December our readers from around the world select the **Story of the Year by casting their votes** for the best of the 12 Story of the Month winners.

WINNERS PRIZES ... WEEKLY, MONTHLY, YEARLY

The 52 Weekly Winners receive the e-book edition of You Can EXPECT A MIRACLE ... The

Book to Change Your Life.

The **Monthly Winners** receive the e-book editions of the next 6 You Can EXPECT A MIRACLE books ... Unexpected Miracles, Yes YOU Can, Insights Into Life, 201 Miracle Messages from A to Z, 13 Keys to Becoming a Miracle Magnet, With Chiropractic.

The **Yearly Winner** will receive the **Story of the Year "Miracle Award" special trophy** as #1 ranking miracle story of the year.

Visit our Website

www.expectamiracle.com

If you know someone who has a heartfelt or dynamite story to tell, please pass the website address on to them and invite them to join us in energizing the mental, emotional and spiritual health of people around the world.

I would appreciate you emailing your address book about this amazing site, and please ask your friends and colleagues to spread the positivity.

Thanks in advance.

If you register on the website, you will receive our **Expect a Miracle Monthly Newsletter ... "The Miracle Messenger".**

The Prestigious Story of the Year "Miracle Award"

Each December, our readers from around the world select the **Story of the Year by casting their votes** for the best of the 12 Story of the Month winners.

The **Yearly Winner** will receive the **Story of the Year "Miracle Award" special trophy** as #1 ranking miracle story of the year, and will be featured on the website and in 'The Miracle Messenger' newsletter.

Simply submit your miracle story into the appropriate category on the website or email your story to: admin@expectamriacle.com

Each week our readers choose a story of the week, **"Readers' Choice Story of the Week".**

Not only are there hundreds of **written stories** you can browse and enjoy, there are also endless numbers of **video stories** you can watch and feel the raw emotion of individuals sharing their miracles.

Looking for a Speaker for Your Next Conference, Seminar or Workshop?

You can contact Dr John Hinwood at john@expectamiracle.com for speaking engagements.

Dr Scott Walker, the Founder of Neuro Emotional Technique from California, USA wrote this note after I spoke to his seminar group about *Expecting Miracles* in November 2007.

"I was attending a *NET SUCCESS* Chiropractic Seminar in Northern New South Wales, Australia. Dr John Hinwood was presenting to the group and asked if there were any volunteers from this group of over 100 chiropractors who would be willing to share a miracle they had witnessed in their lives.

As is typical in such a group, a few brave souls who were not afraid of speaking in public got up and shared some miracles they had seen. Fair enough so far. Most of the attendees said nothing, but applauded the doctors who did share. Then Dr Hinwood asked the audience if they would write down any miracles they had witnessed on a piece of paper.

I was overwhelmed. Why? Without an iota of hesitancy, every single one of the hundred attendees immediately put pen to paper to write about a miracle they had witnessed. There was no pondering or scratching of heads wondering how to phrase things, but an instant and ongoing flow of written descriptions. Apparently, miracles were not hard to come by!

Imagine over one hundred people being able to recall a miracle they had witnessed at the drop of a hat. It appeared that each of them could have come up with several miracles. That so many people were instantly able to recount one miracle was and is miraculous in its own right."

Dr John Hinwood

Expect A Miracle

PO Box 4125

Forest Lake Qld 4078

Australia

Phone:+ 61 3879 0069

Fax: +61 7 3714 9700

Email: admin@expectamiracle.com

Website: www.expectamiracle.com

To Order Additional Copies of this Book

If you would like to order additional copies of this book, either single copies or volume quantities for gift giving, please email us at info@expectamiracle.com or visit us at www.expectamiracle.com.

About the Author

Dr John Hinwood is an author, international speaker, mentor, coach and consultant. His time is spent writing books in the You Can EXPECT A MIRACLE series, speaking to audiences around the world and training, coaching and mentoring a selected groups and clients.

John Hinwood started his career in the 1960s as a physical education high school teacher in Australia, England and South Africa before commencing his Chiropractic studies in Canada in the mid-1970s. He spent a season as the Captain/Coach of the Danish National Rugby team in 1970.

With his wife Judy, he travelled extensively all over the world off the beaten track from 1969 to 1973, overland from Australia through Asia and on to Europe. They spent time in Eastern Europe and Russia during the Cold War. They drove their Land Rover trans-Africa and then spent many months travelling by public transport all over South America and the Caribbean before arriving in Toronto, Canada in the fall of 1973.

In late 1978, John and Judy returned to Australia and set up chiropractic practices in rural communities initially and then in Brisbane, capital of Australia's sunshine state.

In 1985 after eighteen years of marriage, John

and Judy went to Chile and found three older children, Shavela, Ignacio and Rodrigo, in orphanages, whom they then adopted to have an instant family.

John Hinwood now acts as the Coaches Mentor at The Centre for Powerful Practices, which he founded with his wife Judy in 1991. He has an extensive client base worldwide, and publishes a weekly newsletter called *Practice Pointers*, which is e-mailed to over 20,000 practitioners around the world. He has published seven books on chiropractic practice management and numerous multi-media packages.

He has received many awards from chiropractic organisations around the world and is the recipient of the Parker International Award (2003) and Parker International Humanitarian Award (2008) for his services to the chiropractic profession worldwide. He is a Fellow of the International College of Chiropractors (FICC), the Australasian College of Chiropractors (FACC) and the Australian Institute of Management (FAIM). In late 2009, he was made a Life Member of the Chiropractors' Association of Australia and the Australian Spinal Research Foundation for his tireless contribution to his profession and research.

In 2007, he founded Expect A Miracle School Pty Ltd, a company whose sole purpose is to spread the joy of miracles around the world. In November 2007, www.expectamiracle.com went online to provide a forum on the World Wide Web to allow people to continually post and share miracle stories 24 hours a day.

John is a health professional by training, a successful businessman by effort and an inspiration by nature has given him an awesome array of practical tools for success.

As an international speaker, he inspires his audiences into taking practical action steps to move their lives to new levels. His perspectives, humor, observations, insights into life and entertaining stories are from the heart, and they inspire and motivate people into taking positive action steps.

Print Your Own Expect a Miracle Cards

I started this mission of handing out these cards over twenty five years ago, and they have changed my life and the lives of thousands of people with the very simple, yet extremely powerful use of three amazing words. Hope is something we all need continually throughout our lives.

The amazing positive stories and outcomes as a result of people receiving these cards and then creating a miracle through their awareness and shift in consciousness needs to be shared with the broader community. As messengers of hope in the community, we enhance people's lives by supporting all those we come in contact with to experience enhanced physical, mental, emotional and spiritual wellbeing.

Using these little cards as gifts can change YOUR life and the lives of many people you come in contact with during your daily interactions in life.

The power in the card is that it does not have your name on it. It's not about you. It's about the receiver Expecting A Miracle! If you want to spread this message of hope and positivity, then print your own cards so that you can start handing them out.

Many people have asked me over the years if they could copy the idea, and I've said,

"Absolutely, please do!"

The card looks like this, and it is blank on the other side.

> # Expect A Miracle

An easy way to print your own cards is to go to our companion website

www.expectamiracle.com

Go to the link in the footer on the homepage that says Expect A Miracle Cards and email the template to yourself so you can print off your own cards on your home or office printer or email the template to your printer and start handing cards out.

All you need to do is print them from the PDF page that is set out ready for you to use. Print the cards on 350 gsm (or thicker) card stock coated on one side and matt on the blank side. The font used on these cards is my personally designed font, so use the PDF available on the website to print your cards from. The best colour is reflex blue.

Your other choice is to email the PDF file to your printer and supply the printer with the following information: the Expect A Miracle cards are printed on 350 gsm Cast Coat stock or similar (gloss on one side and matt on the other). The blue is Pantone 281c, which is printed digitally with breakdown c100, m72, y0, k32.

Make sure you leave the back of the card blank. Having only the three words "Expect A Miracle" on the card gives it awesome power.

Never doubt that a small group of thoughtful people could change the world.

Indeed, it's the only thing that ever has.

Margaret Mead

Create Miracles For Others ...
Give the Gift of
You Can ... EXPECT A MIRACLE

Available on www.amazon.com or
www.expectamiracle.com

Pure Inspiration ...

Share the Gift of a Book

Available on www.amazon.com or
www.expectamiracle.com

One Last Thing ...

I would like to thank you for taking the time to read this book. I am sincerely grateful and hope that it has lit a fire of inspiration in you to begin to take the steps necessary to live the fullest, most vibrant life you can!

If this book has touched you personally, made you laugh (or maybe cry!), challenged your thinking, sparked inspiration and hope, provided useful information or has made you think of a friend or family member who could do with this kind of information ...

Please, Please, Please...

Take a few minutes to rate this book. When you turn the page, Kindle will give you the opportunity to do this and to share your thoughts on Facebook, LinkedIn and Twitter. If you believe the book is worth sharing, please take a few seconds to let as many people as possible know about it. This is one small step of service you can take to spread the word.

If it turns out to make a difference in peoples lives, they'll be forever grateful to you, as will I.

Once again, my sincerest gratitude and thanks and best of luck on your journey!

Love & miracles

John Hinwood

www.ingramcontent.com/pod-product-compliance
Lightning Source LLC
Chambersburg PA
CBHW061648040426
42446CB00010B/1648

9780987280510